Depth Perception

By

Michael J. Mondl

This book is a work of fiction. Places, events, and situations in this story are purely fictional. Any resemblance to actual persons, living or dead, is coincidental.

ISBN: 1-4033-8916-0 (e-book)
ISBN: 1-4033-8917-9 (Paperback)

This book is printed on acid free paper.

1stBooks - rev. 11/04/02

For Mary

Chapter 1

He raised his fingers to the thick transparent barrier separating himself from the deep and dark interminable void.

The void – endless and eternal.

John VanDeese was alive.

At least that was what they tried to tell him.

His hand met the glass and yet he felt nothing – not the cold, not even the smooth surface itself. He didn't feel anything. That was the whole crux of the problem. He was alive and yet dead inside.

Cold and empty – like the void.

He pressed his body forward and began to merge with the clear thick glass itself, the transparent barrier giving way to his body allowing him to pass right through.

And still he felt nothing. Nothing at all.

It was much too long after the accident to feel sorrow and remorse – too removed from that time and place to feel anger or regret.

He didn't feel alive. He didn't feel anything at all.

His fingers reached the other side of the barrier to the cold dark vacuum of space. He leaned forward and eased more of his arm through up to the elbow, the glass wall rippling like a pool of clear liquid yielding to his flesh. Soon he was completely immersed in the clear barrier . . . part of it . . . one with it. It yielded easily to his body allowing him to transgress on through to the other side.

He was now one with the infinite – the unfeeling limitless expanse of space. For that was their single common denominator – the grounds for a kinship and a bond, as well as a bondage. Both were emptiness, save for tiny specks of white fire nearly extinguished by blackness. There was very little life – only a vast, bleak expanse of dust and cold.

His body drifted in space, tumbling and rolling effortlessly. He turned a slow somersault, watching his spacecraft move slowly away. He felt no remorse, no sense of loss or pain.

He felt nothing at all.

He was now free to be totally and utterly alone – alone with his thoughts . . . alone with his memories.

Alone.

He was floating – free of his painful past, his uncertain future. Part of the void. A kinship – a bondage.

The ship drifted further away until it became just another speck among the twinkling stars and then was gone. He was alone, and yet the misery and despair still remained.

Captain Jonathan VanDeese stood alone in *Hypatia's* observation room, his unseeing eyes staring blankly into the endless infinite vacuum as he struggled to suppress the growing depression that was slowly building inside him. He raised a hand to actually touch the transparent barrier, yet withdrew his fingers before they made contact with the cool glass somehow surmising that giving validity to the portal would force his mind to accept that it was real and therefore destroy the illusion.

Everything in life seemed so futile now. It was all his fault. He should have been with her . . . he should have prevented –

Two years after they were married, his beloved Jennifer had drowned while swimming alone in the ocean, apparently pulled too far out by a strong undercurrent. She was the main source of light in his life, a ray of sunshine cutting through the darkness and the gloom. But that beautiful light had winked out, leaving his soul to exist in the shadows.

At times like these the loneliness and depression grew so intense that the ache became a tangible thing, as a burn upon his flesh. He had heard of cases where people, upon losing a limb, sometimes continued to feel sensations in the missing part as though they had never lost it. However, in his case, John perceived that it was his very soul that had been removed. He swore he could still feel its presence yet knew it no longer existed. In these moments John VanDeese wished he could step through the transparent barrier separating him from the boundless depths of space and merge his body with the cold darkness beyond.

May 4th, 2188. The third anniversary of their marriage.

Would have been.

The captain continued gazing out of the wall-length observation window and tried to make sense of her death and for his continued living. After Jennifer's death he realized his life was lacking purpose and direction. VanDeese admitted that losing Jennifer was his main reason for volunteering to undertake this present mission. *Polaris III:* to deliver a fully functional ice-mining outpost to a moon of Jupiter. It was insanity – piloting a veritable city through the heart of the asteroid belt that lay beyond the planet Mars. Suicide. A crazy mission commanded by a broken man who had nothing to lose. Had he volunteered, or was he chosen? He couldn't remember, nor did he care. He wanted to get as far away from Earth as possible, to literally distance himself from anything that would remind him of his first and only love.

That was the whole essence of the issue – to escape the agonizing torture or to flee and hide one's self away. One had to embrace one's demons or become consumed by them. Either that or run away as far as possible and pray the demons never find you. Just keep running and running to the furthest reaches of the stars.

This was the farthest he had ever been in space, or for any of the passengers and crew aboard his ship for that matter. VanDeese found it more than a little disquieting to be unable to see the Earth from any window or view screen. But then, that was what he had wanted – or so he thought.

He had survived the tragedy and that was what really mattered and he could continue with his life. Yet he was not convinced. If only he wasn't so utterly and totally alone. Every person he had ever loved – his mother, his father, his beautiful Jennifer – all gone. His mind searched for words of comfort to lend meaning to tragedy, purpose to helplessness but none came. There was no meaning or purpose for the pain.

The limitless expanse of space stretched into infinity beyond observation window.

Which way is up?

Funny, the things that would spin through a person's mind as it struggled to keep from wallowing in its own misery. His mother used to read him that poem when he was a little boy. *Which way is up?* It was a nearly-forgotten pleasantry buried deep in the back of his mind that had possibly nurtured his earliest desires to explore the unknowns of space.

Somersault, cartwheel,
Roll like a ball,
I never stand up, I never can fall.
The Earth is below me, now it's above –
Which way is up?

He did not wish this agony of bitter loss inside of him to vanish, for it gave proof that he was still able to feel. Yet this tiny consolation refused him comfort, for why bother to exhibit emotions when his soul was beyond caring for anyone or even for himself? He longed to be part of the void outside, the bleak, empty nothingness. He and space were one. A kinship.

Blackness – measureless and absolute.

Lost in his self-pitying reverie, the captain did not hear the door slide open behind him, nor the soft footsteps approaching on the carpet. "Breathtaking," murmured a deep, throaty woman's voice behind him, the sound barely above a whisper.

Startled, VanDeese jerked his head around to see Doctor Katarina Tushala standing off to his left. The dark, stately statuesque woman was the project's Stellar Cartographer with an additional degree in Cosmochemistry. The captain often wondered why the scientists who were selected for the *Polaris III* mission possessed multiple degrees in a wide range of specialties. It was most likely to minimize the personnel needed for the operation, and therefore the number of persons at risk in this speculative and potentially dangerous project. Tushala was a tall and slender Israeli woman with short, raven-black hair, tan skin and sharp features. She was nearly as tall as the captain, and stood close enough to VanDeese that he could actually feel the heat radiating from her body. And there was heat – it wasn't merely a machination of his imagination. The black satiny material of her one-piece jumpsuit accentuated the woman's lean lithe figure so acutely that it clung to her body like a second skin, revealing more details of her anatomy than the fabric managed to conceal. She might just as well be wearing nothing at all, which may have been the illusion she was trying to achieve.

"It can be strangely compelling," VanDeese agreed, returning his gaze to the void beyond the glass. He briefly wondered if they were both speaking about the stars.

Tushala stepped closer, her thinly-concealed breasts brushing gently against the captain's sleeve. Katarina wore no undergarments beneath her tight form-fitting spandex jumpsuit, the satiny black material acutely accenting each curve and valley of her willowy physique. Her snug wardrobe was quite a stark contrast of his own loose powder blue uniform. Then again, the woman was a passenger not a member of his crew. She could wear anything she wanted or nothing at all, and from the looks of it the woman had settled for a compromise of both.

"Ever since I was a young girl," Katarina breathed throatily. "I stared at the stars and knew that they held the last mysteries. How many stars were there? How many planets like ours, I wondered?" She turned her face to his. "I guess I had always known that my future lay among the stars." She stood so close that their bodies nearly pressed against one another. VanDeese wasn't quite certain if this was a normal posture for her, if it was just her way of being friendly. Or was she being intentionally alluring?

When the captain first met Doctor Tushala before their departure from space dock, he had guessed that most men probably found her type sensuous and mysterious. Her voice was a low throaty purr like the deep growl of an immense jungle feline. She had a disturbing way of looking at a man as an animal might size up its prey with her steady, almost probing, constant gaze. Her deep, penetrating dark eyes through half-lowered lids had a way of making VanDeese feel more than a little uncomfortable. When the woman walked, she carried herself with the poise and grace of one with regal position and authority. She had a lean and sinewy body that stimulated primal desires in men, causing their minds to fantasize endless hours of wild wanton abandon, exploring the abundant pleasures of incredibly satisfying sexual expression. John wondered if she knew or was even aware that she affected men in such a provocative fashion. He suspected that she made a game of demanding attention to her body with her graceful stride and provocative posture, arousing men with each practiced gesture and enticing movement.

"Have you ever felt that?" Katarina asked. "That you have a destiny?"

"No," he answered the window coolly taking a step away from the woman.

Katarina moved behind him and wrapped her slender arms around his waist. The captain stiffened reflexively, a nanosecond of surprise and sudden tension at the unexpected embrace. Doctor Tushala released her hold and shifted to his side to study his face a moment. "I apologize if I did something wrong."

"No no . . . I was just . . . startled, that's all."

"You want I should leave?"

VanDeese turned from her and sat in one of the observation chairs. He casually crossed his legs and looked at his hands in his lap. "Leave? Why? Whatever for?"

"I seem to be making you uncomfortable."

The captain raised his eyes to the wide window. "No. You caught me at a bad moment. Reminiscing about something . . . about someone."

"A woman?"

He looked back at his lap and picked at an invisible piece of lint on his slacks. The woman silently glided into the seat beside him. "Tell me."

"My wife," VanDeese sighed. "Her name was Jennifer. She died almost a year ago."

Katarina fell silent for a moment. "That's a long time for a man to grieve."

He turned his face to her. He didn't particularly enjoy this session of psychoanalysis. "Is psychology one of your many degrees?"

The doctor leaned back in her seat and looked at him sideways. "I know that for a man to be without companionship for that long is not good." She leaned toward him and gently caressed his cheek with the backs of her fingers. "Continue with your life." VanDeese stood abruptly and took a step away. "You won't be paying her any disrespect by continuing with your life," Tushala urged. VanDeese remained silent. "What was the old expression?" she paused, tilting her head to one side. "If you fall from your horse . . ."

"Doctor Tushala, this isn't quite as simple – "

"Kat," she interrupted."

"I beg your pardon?"

"Call me Kat," she smiled demurely. "Since we're going to be close travelling companions aboard this small vessel for such a long time I suggest we get to know each other on more friendlier terms. Don't you agree, John?"

The tiny electronic *sponder* implant in his ear canal chirped twice and VanDeese cocked his head as if someone were talking over his shoulder. "Captain here," he responded to the wall.

"Hey, Johnny-o," Ron's voice exploded in his ear. It sounded as though the chief engineer were standing right behind the captain's shoulder. "I've made some adjustments to the little lady's *HIPS* and I wanted to show you the latest results on her performance."

John VanDeese drew in, then expelled a long sigh. "Sure Ron. I'll be down in a little while."

His old friend cleared his throat after a brief but awkward silence. "I realize what day it is. If you want to have a drink or something later . . ."

"Yeah sure," VanDeese acknowledged listlessly. "Thanks."

Ron Saint was not only the ship's engineer but also the captain's oldest and dearest friend. He was VanDeese's Best Man at his wedding and one of the few who were able to attend Jennifer's funeral.

"Incoming call?" Kat smirked crossing her long sinewy legs at the knees. "Or are you just pretending so you can escape from me?"

He turned to her. "Escape?"

"Running away."

"You don't appear to be all that threatening to me." It was clear the woman had no concealed weapons anywhere on her person.

"Oh, I don't know," she leered, crossing her arms under her bosom. "Some people think I'm dangerous as hell. Women especially."

"I'm not afraid of you."

"You most certainly are," she laughed, rising to her feet and walking over to the observation window. "You're afraid I may make you forget about her – if even for an instant."

The captain remained silent, his eyes following the smooth satiny contours of her cat-like physique. He had no doubt this woman could make any man forget every woman but her. But most likely the chase would hold more excitement than the capture to this sultry lioness leaving her prey feeling used and more hollow than before.

Katarina gazed silently at the passing stars, her finger absently rubbing the spot behind her ear where the implant had been inserted in her ear canal. "At first I was a little apprehensive about having one of these devices placed inside my head," she mused dreamily.

"I was afraid people would be able to read my mind . . . my thoughts."

"It's perfectly safe," the captain assured. "It's for communicating only."

"Oh I'm not worried about it any more," she said, turning to him. "In fact, I oftentimes forget it's even there." She moved a step closer to him. "There are times when I wouldn't mind having a man read my thoughts."

"I'm fairly certain I can read them now," he admitted candidly.

Kat grinned. "Sometimes my self-expression is a little less than subtle."

"I'll grant you that."

"But my intentions are genuine. I'm not looking for a long meaningful relationship. Just a little – *satisfaction* – to sate my physical needs."

"What do you mean?"

Tushala threw her head back and laughed out loud. "Oh darling, please!"

The captain flushed slightly and turned away. "If you'll excuse me," he coughed. "I'm needed in engineering."

"You're needed here." She stepped closer, crowding the commander against the wall. "Don't you find me attractive?" she demanded suddenly.

VanDeese was momentarily caught off guard. "Attractive? Why, yes . . . absolutely."

"Sleep with me then."

"*What*?"

"You know . . . *Sex*? Man and a woman? Don't tell me it's been *that* long for you."

"I haven't really thought – "

"Of course you have," she smirked, crowding him closer, her breasts brushing the front of his tunic. "Probably as recent as a few moments ago."

"You certainly are a direct woman."

Katarina smiled cattily and tilted her head to one side, her eyes lowering slightly. "And why not? There's only the two of us here. Besides, it may be just the kind of release that is needed . . . for *both* of us."

"I'm flattered, but – "

"Relax, darling," she interrupted, raising a hand to his face. "It isn't my intention to make you uncomfortable. Quite the reverse. You'll feel much better after you've made love with a willing and able partner. I know I will. Believe me, I need this as much as you do."

"Perhaps now is not the time."

"Later then," she cooed, her fingers sliding lower over his chest. "My cabin?"

VanDeese awkwardly cleared his throat. "That is certainly something worth considering. Now if you'll excuse me." The captain turned to leave but was quickly stopped by the woman gripping his elbow and pulled his body back toward her. "You're not trying to avoid me, are you darling?"

"Avoid you?"

Tushala eased her grasp and gently stroked the captain's arm. "We've been aboard this ship for over two weeks now and this is the first time we've been alone together." She slid her fingers down his arm and raised the back of his hand to her cheek. "Are you afraid of me?" she mewed demurely.

"Afraid? Of course not."

"You said you find me attractive."

"Well . . . yes."

She flicked her tongue out, softly licking his knuckles. "Stimulating?"

"Kat . . . "

"*Arousing?*"

VanDeese felt his face reddening and slowly drew his hand away. "Doctor Tushala . . . *Kat* . . . this probably isn't the time or place – "

Katarina stepped close, her hot body pressing tightly against the captain's chest as she hooked her arms around his neck. "Wrong on both counts." She pulled his face closer to hers, her lips pressing long and hard onto his. Her mouth burned upon his with a heat from – what was it? Not lust or passion. *Examination.* Analysis. Research. She was finding out whether she was having an effect upon him and to what extent her efforts caused him to become aroused. Always the scientist, studying cause and effect. Stimulus and response.

After a few moments she withdrew and regarded VanDeese through half-lowered eyelids. The captain drew in his breath to speak and she silenced him with a finger to his lips. "Yes darling, I know," she sighed. "You're needed in engineering."

"Yes."

"Playing hard to get has its boundaries," she breathed lustfully. "A woman can remain patient just so long."

"We'll be on board a while longer," he added stepping back a little. "I'm sure there will be other opportunities to discuss the matter of your needs – "

"My needs – *our* needs – "

"Exactly."

"Perhaps when you are not otherwise engaged," she purred, "we could arrange to meet somewhere more . . . *private*." She allowed her hands to slide slowly down John's face and neck. "I am sure that we could discover several things of . . . *mutual* interest." Her finger slowly began to draw little symbols on his chest.

VanDeese watched the movements of her finger for a short while, then lifted his eyes to her beautiful smiling face. "Yes . . . well . . . that would be quite . . . enjoyable." John took a step back and bowed his head slightly. "Until then." He turned and crossed the room to the door, trying not to leave too quickly. He could hear Tushala's breath coming in a deep chuckle behind him. The captain couldn't believe the woman had practically thrown herself at him in such a forward manner. Even worse, he couldn't believe he had brushed her off so quickly beating a hasty retreat. Perhaps Kat was right, a night of mad passionate abandon may be just what he needed but not on this day. *Their day*. VanDeese was too submerged in his own self-pity and despair to allow himself any pleasures – physical or otherwise.

He stopped to compose himself in the corridor as he waited for the *tube* to arrive. The *tube* was more than an elevator, it was a cylinder pulled by air pressure through a network of conduits throughout the structure of the ship. VanDeese stepped in and the door slid silently behind him.

Tushala was right, he was running away. He realized that he had been fooling himself into believing that the time of grieving was over. And he *was* running. Running away from women, from life, even from himself. He and Jennifer had been a rare combination, one that only came along once – if ever – in a lifetime. They were truly fortunate to find one another, which made the wrenching separation even more devastating and unbearable. Of course, he had established platonic friendships with several women since the tragedy, but not with the openness and affection he once felt, the affection he assured himself he was no longer able to give. He convinced himself that he just wasn't ready. Not yet. It wouldn't be fair to Katarina or to himself to enter into a relationship – if even for one night – while his mind was still occupied by another woman. That was why VanDeese avoided any familiar encounters or lasting relationships with women. He knew that he could never find love as meaningful as his first had been. He continued to run away, shying from life's good experiences to avoid the bad.

Running and hiding.

Continue with your life she said.

What life?

Once inside the *tube* the captain expelled his breath in a long heavy sigh. If he were more prone to physical outbursts he might have slammed his fists against the hard metal walls and cursed his misfortune. He hadn't even enough emotion left inside him for a good cry. Still, it would not do to have the captain of a starship be seen all teary-eyed and weepy, even if he was mourning the loss of a loved one.

"Engineering."

He forced his mind to suppress his emotions once again and focus on the mission at hand. It was, after all, the only thing he had left in his life worth caring about.

Chapter 2

The engineering department was a suite of several rooms, primarily containing technical equipment arranged in banks of displays, gauges, meters, buttons and switches. One room held several computer consoles for running simulations. Another was mostly a stockpile of tools and fixtures for maintenance and ship repair. Ron Saint's office was at the far end of this labyrinth of equipment. He specifically designed this layout of rooms so that his visitors would be awed by the extent of the technological marvel and all the factors that went into its design and construction. It was *his* ship, and it gave *The Saint* a feeling of pride and satisfaction in letting everyone know the extent of his genius.

Most of the people within the aeronautics and scientific community who either knew or heard of the man affectionately referred to him as *The Saint*. He had become something of a living legend whose name was whispered with veneration in halls of academies and universities. Ron had been one of four technicians in a laboratory that was suddenly ripped by a freak explosion. One scientist was killed instantly, but Ron had managed to drag the two others from the burning wreckage. This act of heroism was all the more incredible as the explosion had badly mutilated and burned his left arm. The limb was beyond restoration, and had to be replaced by a cybernetic mechanical implant. One couldn't tell any differences from the look of it, but the artificial arm was far stronger and more sensitive than a real limb. Losing his arm did little to quell the engineer's amiable personality, taking the operation in stride and accepting the loss of a limb as merely an opportunity for inner growth. Throughout his recovery and physical therapy, Ron's attitude remained positive, and he continued to be instrumental in the development of new and improved astronautic technology.

As a condition of accepting command of the ship, VanDeese insisted that Ron accompany him as Chief Engineer. It was not a surprising request, since *The Saint* was involved in *Hypatia's* design and personally supervised throughout the construction of the ship. Indeed, many of its circuits, systems and component specifications were of his own creation. Ron knew more about *Hypatia's* internal workings than any other person alive. But because of his physical disability, it was impossible to offer him any military rank, leaving *The Saint* the only civilian member of the captain's four-member crew. Ron was permitted to participate in the voyage merely as an advisor with no authority for command, nor could he make any executive decisions. Nonetheless, all the members of the crew and their scientist passengers heeded his advice regarding the ship's operation and maintenance. To do otherwise would be not only foolish and stupid, but the offender may also find himself pitted against the quick-witted engineer in mental combat; a contest that even the scientists agreed they would most likely lose.

Ron had his bed moved into the engineering office, for it was there that he spent most of his time anyway. He had his own cabin, but it was used primarily for storage of technical manuals, design upgrades, alteration documentation, and the recorded lectures of his scientific contemporaries. There was no need for hard manuals or reference materials in the engineering department. Once *The Saint* had read or viewed the information, it was immediately and permanently logged into the data archives of his brain. This phenomenon never ceased to amaze the captain. All facts, figures and formulas were stored in the man's quick mind as neatly and economically as any computer database.

As VanDeese entered the engineering department, he heard a man's voice to his left, hidden behind a computer console. The voice was soothing and caressing.

"Oh baby, yeah! Come on, just a little more. That's it! Yes! *YES!*"

If it were anyone else's voice he'd heard, the captain might have quietly stepped back into the lift, embarrassed at having intruded upon an intimate scene. But VanDeese had witnessed the engineer speaking to his engines in such a way before, and he accepted it as a quirky part of *The Saint*'s personality.

VanDeese mused that it was strange, this odd love affair between an engineer and his ship, which Ron had dubbed *Hypatia*. This was a word play on *H.I.P.S.*, which stood for the *Hawking Inductive Propulsion System*, named after the twentieth-century scientist Stephen Hawking, whose theories of physics and the universe revolutionized the way modern scientists looked upon space and space travel.

Hypatia's high-efficiency solar collecting panels converted sunlight into magnetic energy through the huge inductive coils in the ship's port and starboard nacelles. The magnetic field induced by the coils would literally bend space, allowing the ship to move as if riding along the crest of a wave. By varying the amount of power to either cell, the ship could turn, stop or reverse. The *HIPS* drive was prohibited from atmospheric use because the tremendous force and turbulence created by the magnetic fields would cause abrupt air currents and atmospheric disturbances. The sub-zero temperature of space was ideal, insuring the coils of minimal heat loss, and actually increasing their performance.

The *HIPS* drive was revolutionary in its design and function. Its use of solar power was more economical than liquid or solid fuels. At maximum speed it could propel a craft at the mind-staggering velocity of 9800 km per second. Allowing for the drop in speed necessary for passing through the asteroid belt, the journey would require a little over 45 days to reach their destination of Ganymede, a moon of Jupiter.

The Saint had never been married. In fact, VanDeese could not recall him ever having a girlfriend for that matter. It wasn't so unusual, he thought, for brainy engineering types rarely clouded their thinking with matters of the heart.

Ron was a personable enough man – always the first to help when needed, often going out of his way to make sure a birthday or anniversary wasn't forgotten. VanDeese surmised he just regarded women as coworkers and friends, treating them as equals. "I prefer to live out my fantasies through you," he once told the captain. "It's safer, cleaner, and my creative mind can substitute more lewd scenarios for the dull spots."

Ron looked up from the computer display when he heard his visitor approaching. "Hey, Johnny-boy. Look! I found a way to coax another 2.047 percent of power from the inductive conversion conduits by rerouting a portion of the stream to a network traversing the hull along the axis at the keel."

The captain looked from the console readouts to the engineer and gave a fractional shrug of his shoulders. VanDeese didn't even try to understand all the mechanics of the propulsion, artificial gravity and maneuvering mechanisms that were incorporated into the fundamentals of the *HIPS* drive. He had Ron with him, and that was enough.

"Don't you see?" *The Saint* asked incredulously. "The power transfer is nearly 96 percent efficient, which means only 4 percent of her energy is dissipated through heat loss!"

VanDeese allowed a small smile. "I really think you could use a little time off for recreation."

"Hardy har har."

The captain furrowed his brow. "Hardy what?"

"Forget it."

"Look, Ron, if you find yourself having lurid dreams about your beloved *Hypatia*, I'm sure one of our scientific passengers would enjoy giving you some private psychological counseling." He could think of one spandex-clad female scientist in particular.

Ron leaned back in his chair and scowled, crossing his arms across his chest. "You're a fine one to talk," he grumbled. "Dragging yourself around here for the last few days, about as much fun as a wet sock."

VanDeese pulled a chair over and straddled it backwards, crossing his arms on the backrest. "I know," he sighed. "I thought that getting away from everything would help me to forget."

"But you made the mistake of bringing yourself along," Ron drawled. *The Saint*'s features relaxed slightly. "It's been eleven months, John. Time to get on with your life."

"Continue with your life," he grunted.

"Exactly."

The captain rested his chin on his arms and closed his eyes. "You ever get lonely, Ron?" The engineer uncrossed his arms and regarded his friend sadly. "I mean, so damn lonely that you picture a single moment frozen in time inside your head and wish with every fiber of your soul that it would remain there and last forever." VanDeese opened his eyes and looked at Ron. "You ever get that way?"

"Jenny's dead, John."

"I know."

"Look, you can either wallow in your little pity party or be grateful for the time you had together and get on with your life."

"That simple, huh?" VanDeese sighed.

"Take me for example," the engineer said, extending his left arm. "I could have let this get me down, but I didn't. You take the punches and keep on moving. Life goes on."

"It's not the same."

"What, losing a part of you? Something you took for granted, never thinking for one moment that something might happen that would change you forever? Well, maybe it's not the same, but it makes you appreciate what you have, knowing that nothing is eternal."

VanDeese expelled his breath in a long sigh and looked up at the ceiling. "You ever think you'll ever find the right person for you, Ron?"

"Nah," he shrugged. "I'll probably just build the perfect woman out of spare parts."

"You would." The two men fell silent for a few moments. "I went to the observation room on level seven," VanDeese continued in a faraway voice, his eyes averted to the floor. "I sometimes go there when I feel depressed. I thought looking out into the endless emptiness of space would place myself in a proper perspective, to see how tiny my anxieties really were." He looked back at his friend. "This time it didn't work. The universe just wasn't big enough."

"Boy, you really got it bad." Ron opened a drawer in his desk and pulled out a transparent flask of dark liquid and two short glasses. "I stashed this on board for just such an occasion. Genuine 70-proof whiskey." He poured a small amount into each glass and handed one to the captain. "It may not help you to forget, but it might break you out of your melancholy mood."

VanDeese sat up straight and eyed his glass dubiously. "Not synthetic?"

"Nope. The real thing."

The captain sighed. "Just don't say, *Happy Anniversary*."

The engineer laughed. "How about 'Today is the first day of the rest of your life?'"

"Better." He extended his hand and clinked the glass in his friend's hand.

John VanDeese walked slowly through a row of Sycamore and Maple trees with his hands clasped behind his back. He kept his eyelids partially closed, breathing in deeply the smell of the fresh green vegetation. *Jenny would have loved it here* he thought, stopping and raising his eyes to the limbs of a towering Elm nearly ten meters in height. The light filtering through the branches was bright but not blinding. There was no wind and the temperature was comfortable. All of his surroundings were pleasant and relaxing, unlike the cold and unfeeling vastness of space.

He swore that after all those years of shuttle-runs carrying personnel and supplies to the installations on Earth's moon bases that he would no longer accept journeys away from his home planet. He promised his new wife Jennifer that he was going to give it all up and that he would take a safe, administrative position close to home so that he could remain near to her. But Jennifer was no longer there to make sure he kept his promise, and VanDeese returned to the life he knew best, the job he performed so well.

VanDeese accepted this latest mission because of the distance it involved. It would take him far away from Earth, as far into space as any human had ever gone. The project coordinators allowed him to personally choose his crew of three other persons who would escort a veritable city and its five scientists to establish an ice-mining operation on Ganymede, one of moons of Jupiter. The project was initiated to supplement the Earth's dwindling water supply. Due to industrial pollution, contamination and higher demands for fresh water, the Earth's filtration and reclamation facilities were finding it more and more difficult to meet the world's requirements. Earth's governmental agencies had explored the possibility of extracting ice from Mars, but the water supply on the Red Planet was extremely limited and so high in mineral content that it proved too costly a venture.

The moon of Jupiter named Ganymede was merely a ball of ice orbiting the huge red planet. A colony established primarily for an excavation operation could mine for centuries and send the ice back to Earth for melting, filtering and distribution. Scientists believed that with a gradual melting process over a long period, the introduction of stellar ice would not affect the Earth's ecosystems and global temperature. Once the mining operation had been established on Ganymede, cargo carriers would make the rounds every six months, bringing supplies and equipment, personnel and mining tools.

All of the crew and scientists had been volunteers, for not only was this project intended to be operating for six months before the next supplying ship would come from Earth, but they would have to navigate through the asteroids and space debris floating in a wide belt between Mars and Jupiter.

The unmanned *Polaris I* and the two-manned ship *Polaris II* were successful in navigating through the band of floating rocks. However, they had been spacecraft of much smaller size and could more easily steer clear around the moving boulders. This project, *Polaris III*, was on a much larger scale. It was literally a flying city, its base covering the area of three square kilometers and rising fifteen stories. The craft's immense bulk would make it much more difficult to avoid smaller and faster moving asteroids. Proposals to navigate above or below the belt were rejected due to round-trip time restrictions and to the bureaucratic confidence in the captain's maneuvering capabilities.

The city had been created spacious enough not only for the design and fabrication of ice-mining equipment, but for the housing of the project's workers, who, at this point, were merely human embryos suspended in a cryogenic state. Cryogenics, or Cryobiological Suspension was the process of preserving organic tissues in chambers that maintained sub-zero temperatures. At the present, it was only used on components of organic bodies such as tissue and organs. Astronautic engineers had considered using Cryogenics for the preservation of adult astronauts on deep-space explorations. However, they had not yet found any suitable mentally-stable volunteers who were willing to undergo the freezing process. Human embryos were acceptable up to a certain stage of development, before the brain became functional. Four thousand such embryos were stored within a special section of the ship. They would be grown only a few at a time, the first in an accelerated state, achieving maturity in several weeks. Consecutive embryos would develop at a less rapid and more normal rate.

Every consumable item within the city would be recycled and reused. The oxygen-to-carbon dioxide ratio of the air was continuously monitored by the city's computer system, the used air being redirected through the Botanical section for the plants to utilize the carbon dioxide. The computer would also release additional oxygen from storage canisters to compensate for population variances. The computer was also capable of shutting down certain sections of ventilation if it needed to reclaim some of the air in those areas. Water would be filtered and purified, with the impurities being sent to an elaborate septic distribution network below the plants and trees for their fertilization. Human waste and uneaten food were also processed by the city's reclamation machinery for the benefit of the plants. There was no garbage, no waste. Everything was either sterilized for reuse or broken down into lesser components and recycled. The cargo carrying ships, making their round-trip voyages from Earth every six months would deliver equipment, personnel and consumables such as extra food, water and air, and then pick up the mined ice for the return trip to earth.

The captain and his crew referred to the entire vessel as their ship, though technically it was two separate components. *Polaris III* was the name given to the ice-mining project, which was essentially the city itself and the main bulk of the craft and would be deposited upon the surface of the ice-moon Ganymede. Extending from the top center of the uppermost level of the city was a conduit ten meters in length, attached to the docking port of the navigation and propulsion craft. This vessel was christened *Hypatia* by its creator as a pun of the anagram of the ship's innovative drive system, the H.I.P.S. drive. *Hypatia* was a narrow, triangular V-shaped craft, much like a slender boomerang with the inductive propulsion nacelles extending horizontally front-to-back from each wing tip. The huge inductive coils within the nacelles would set up a magnetic field, capable of propelling the ship and the city through space. Similar inductive units were situated within various locations throughout the city to provide the artificial gravity and create the navigational shields necessary for the craft's protection on its stellar voyage.

Once the city was secured to the moon's surface, the propulsion craft would disengage from the connecting conduit for its return journey to Earth. Also attached to the roof of the city was a triangular turret connected to two emergency space-pods and a vacant port for the docking of the cargo ships.

Captain VanDeese walked silently along the long rows of flourishing trees. There was every type he could identify and many he could not. He came around the end of a row of Birch trees and saw the legs of a ladder at the base of one tree extending up into the branches. As he drew nearer, he saw the legs of a man on the higher rungs in the branches. It was Doctor Harold Pollack, the project's botanist, who also specialized in microbial physiology. He was examining the leaves with a small hand-held electronic meter.

"Hello Hal," VanDeese called to the scientist. "What's up? Besides you, of course."

Doctor Pollack looked down from between the branches and smiled. He was a short, stocky man in his mid-forties with a rounded face and dark receding hair. A friendly and jovial man, the scientist got along easily with everyone. "Good morning, Captain," he said happily. "Or is it afternoon? With this artificial lighting I can never tell the difference."

"What are you doing up there?" the captain asked, stepping to the base of the ladder.

"Oh, I was just measuring the effects of prolonged exposure to artificial lighting upon the pigmentation of these leaves," the doctor explained.

"Sounds like loads of fun."

"Well, until we reach our destination, I have nothing but time on my hands."

"Don't let me stop you."

"Tell me when we get close to the asteroid belt," Hal said. "I don't think I'd like to be up a tree when you start flipping and twisting us around."

"It'll be a few more hours yet," the captain stated. "I'll let everyone know when they should strap themselves in."

"You make it sound dangerous."

"Nothing to worry about," VanDeese said, though he knew otherwise. Navigating through the asteroid belt would be neither easy or safe. "See you later."

"Goodbye captain." VanDeese headed for the side exit and summoned the tube for the bridge, taking a long look back at the lush greenery he so hurriedly rushed to leave behind on Earth.

Jenny would have loved it here.

Chapter 3

The asteroid belt was still a few hours away. There, VanDeese would be required to navigate the ship around the floating boulders, preferably without destroying *Hypatia* in the process. He still didn't understand why they needed a captain for this mission. Hell, he didn't know why they needed him along at all. Computers have flown ships before. The captain surmised that it all boiled down to the human factor. Computer intelligence still remained somewhat limited and lacking when unforseen circumstances arrived. Like the asteroid belt. A guidance program could traverse the belt in simulation much more efficiently, but throw in a few unexpected twists and it came up short every time.

Vandeese had something of a sixth sense about him in unpredictable situations. His success rate using manual steering controls in computer simulations consistently scored 5 to 10 percent higher than artificial intelligence models.

That was why he was chosen for the mission. Why he was chosen as the captain, and why he would have to navigate the ship manually through the obstacle course of hurtling boulders. Man proved better than the machine in a crisis.

VanDeese would get them through. It was possible.

In theory.

The captain was beginning to grow restless and edgy, as if anticipating and waiting for something but was unable to act.

Hurry up and wait. Or was it wait and hurry up? Something like that. It was an old military expression, the source long forgotten, but still applicable. He hated waiting, his body and mind idle. His father used to say, "Do something – even if it's wrong." VanDeese was a man of action, in a position of command and authority, constrained within in the grip of time and delay.

He decided to pass some of the time chatting with his favorite microbiologist in the city's Cryogenic Suspension area. Cryogenics, or Cryobiological Suspension was the process of preserving organic tissues in chambers that maintained sub-zero temperatures. Presently, it was mainly used on components of organic bodies such as tissue and organs. This was the first space mission where whole beings would be transported a great distance and then raised to maturity after long-term suspension. No one could predict how being raised so far from their mother planet would effect the physiology and mental state of the subjects. For all anyone knew they would be creating a whole new species of humankind.

The project's Microbiologist was named Consuela Garcia, but she preferred to be called Connie. She was a woman in her late-thirties, with bright eyes and a quick wit. Connie was a plump Hispanic woman whose gentle manner and jolly humor made her easily likable and pleasant to associate with. Doctor Garcia's specialty was in Cryogenics and tissue regeneration, but as a government representative, she had to serve the crew as both scientist and ambassador with the tact and personality that were vital in dealing with other departments and bureaucracies. There had been much discussion and argument regarding the practice of "creating people," and Doctor Garcia had been assigned to make sure that everything was done strictly by the book. The care, maintenance and growth of the human embryos were her responsibilities – duties she accepted very seriously. These were not merely embryos to her, they were her children, and she made sure that nobody messed with her kids.

Captain VanDeese found Connie Garcia testing a tissue sample to calibrate and verify some of the readouts from her medical equipment. She constantly monitored all the instruments and systems to ensure that everything remained functioning properly. "Hello there cutie!" she laughed with a wink. "Haven't seen you for a few days. Have you been hiding from me?"

"You're the second woman who's asked me that today," he mumbled. Connie was a flirt, but always in harmless good-natured fun. Under normal circumstances, VanDeese would enjoy her bantering of double entendres and hidden innuendoes, but today he simply wasn't in the mood.

He wandered around the lab and looked through the double glass doors to the Embryonic Storage Chamber. It looked like a huge bank vault: rows and rows of small compartments, each containing a living organism – a human fetus suspended in an early stage of development. Connie jokingly referred to them as "womb-mates." These were not clones or test-tube babies, but the products of unwanted pregnancies – children given up by their natural parents in the hopes that others may provide a better life for their children than they could. Even in the twenty-second century, birth control and teenage pregnancy were still issues of controversy and debate.

"You haven't named them all, have you?" VanDeese chided jokingly, pointing to the storage chamber.

Doctor Garcia chuckled and crossed to her desk. "I've only assigned them numbers for now. I'll give them names that we have entered in a database that should fit their personalities and demeanor as they grow."

The captain looked at the long rows of cryogenically-suspended embryos. "Doesn't the process hurt them?" he frowned.

Connie sat behind her desk. "You mean, can they feel it? I don't think so. At least, I hope not. They're placed into suspension long before any brainwave activity is detected. Also, when I bring them out, I put them into an accelerated generative condition, so that any damaged cells from their hibernation are quickly renewed."

"So just what do you mean by '*accelerated*'?"

Connie leaned forward, resting her elbows on her desk. "The first generation will have a much more rapid growth than succeeding generations," she explained. "By the time the mining operation is ready, the first series – about a dozen or so – will be fully grown. The growth process will take several weeks, in which time the fetuses will receive neural and cerebral stimulation so that they can grow up just as active and intelligent as normal children into adulthood." She frowned for a moment in solemn reflection. "Unfortunately, they won't have any childhood memories. In other words, they will literally be old before their times."

VanDeese dropped heavily into a chair by her desk. "*Dios*," he cursed under his breath. "To think that science can do such things. How can we justify performing such procedures upon human beings?"

Doctor Garcia frowned and looked at her clasped hands. "Man has done worse things to himself and other organisms under the guise of science," she admitted. She ruefully shook her head. "I know I'm not playing God. I'm not *creating* people. I'm just adjusting their speed of development. The succeeding generations will be grown at a much more normal rate."

VanDeese had no qualms with Cryogenic Suspension. The practice had been used for over a century, primarily for the medical treatment of diseases and organ disorders. It was the scientific tampering with human development growth rates that he disliked. He disagreed with the creation of human adults embodying inexperienced – and therefore malleable – naive and childlike minds. "How have children previously grown through this rapid development process coped with the realization that they were now as old or even older than their parents?"

Connie shook her head. "Some didn't. They experienced a genuine lack-of-identity crisis. There's even a medical term for it. It's called AMS: Accelerated Maturity Syndrome. At first their world is wonderful, exploring things with the strength and mobility of an adult. Later, through interaction with adults who have experienced a more normal growth pattern, they discover that they are fundamentally dissimilar. They feel deprived, even robbed of their childhood, which often leads to a state of depression. Sometimes even suicide." She leaned back in her chair. "I doubt we should have such extreme cases here. This is an enclosed environment where all generations will grow up exposed to the same stimulus. Of course, we'll inform them that they are a little different from their 'cousins' on Earth. But at least they won't feel alienated among their peers within this environment." Doctor Garcia pointed to a stasis chamber. "That one on the left is Fernando," she smiled. "He is going to be a chemist when he grows up. And Maria the little *chica* next to him will be an artist."

"I see you've already named some of them," he chuckled.

"Only a few," she nodded playfully. "We can't have them growing up with names like 317XF92 or some other scientific designation like that. They will be real children – they need real names."

"And you've already picked out the types of lives they will lead."

"Simply wishful thinking," she shrugged. "A mother can never tell how her children will turn out."

"That is certainly a fitting description of you, doctor," the captain smiled, patting her hand. "A mother hen watching over her brood." The *sponder* implant in the captain's ear canal chirped. "Excuse me, Connie," he said. "VanDeese here."

"Captain? Lieutenant Soo," the voice returned. "Outer perimeter of asteroid belt in ninety minutes."

"Understood." The captain sighed and rose from his chair. "Got to go."

"So soon?"

"Duty calls."

"Always on duty," she sighed. "I hope you can find time for recreation."

"I'm the captain of a starship," he said dryly.

"Even a captain has to relax," she scowled. Connie stared at him a moment. "John . . . is everything all right?"

VanDeese frowned. "Why do you ask?"

"You seem a little preoccupied and distant." She leaned forward in her chair. "I'm worried about you. I hope you're not overly-anxious about this asteroid-barrier thing."

"It isn't that," he admitted. VanDeese stepped around her desk and rested a hand on Connie's shoulder. "I've just been experiencing a little distress over some personal problems. Nothing to be concerned about."

Connie patted his hand and smiled warmly at him. "I'm here if you need to get something off your chest."

VanDeese nodded. "Thanks." He shook his head wearily. "I came to see you, hoping to break out of this depressed mood I've been in. Instead, I've succeeded in passing some of it on to you."

Connie smiled and waved a hand dismissively. "Forget it. Just deliver us to Ganymede. We'll have plenty of time for laughs later."

"Thanks, Connie. You're a good friend."

"Oh, that's just my maternal nature," she laughed. "Having four thousand children tends to bring it out in me."

Hypatia's bridge was a moderately spacious room with computer readout displays and console stations on three of its walls. The fourth wall was little more than a view screen that spanned its entire length and stretched from floor to ceiling, offering an outside view of their course. It was a liquid-crystal display, and did not give VanDeese the same sense of vertigo that he felt in the observation room. The captain stood nearly spellbound as he stared at the view outside. The boulders were much larger and more numerous than he had previously imagined. "By the eyes of Kohlox," he breathed. "Look at all of them." Only a day before, *Hypatia* was still far enough away that the band of drifting rocks seemed a small, innocuous hurdle to overcome. VanDeese could now see that it was an immense and perilous barrier.

Hypatia used solar energy for power and propulsion, making subsequent trips to the Red Giant's moon swift and cost-effective. Highest hopes were placed upon the ice-mining colony becoming a success – if only VanDeese could deliver it to Ganymede without killing everyone in the process. Earth's unwanted babies would be given new homes and a deep-space observatory would be established to explore the far reaches of the solar system. There were even discussions of Ganymede becoming a springboard for further exploration and future ventures to the outermost planets were in the planning stages. It all hinged upon John VanDeese and his ability to deliver – literally. Proposals to navigate above or below the asteroid belt were rejected due to round-trip time restrictions and from bureaucratic confidence in the captain's maneuvering capabilities. But now, looking at the rock barrier they had to cross, VanDeese wished that he shared their optimism.

VanDeese looked to the upper right of the bridge. Li Soo, his young female science officer was sitting at her console setting its programming to monitor any adverse effects or damage to the ship – either physical abuse from the asteroids or from various types of radiation. She was an attractive Asian woman not quite twenty years of age. Her face and figure suggested that she was most likely descended from an area around the Southeast Asian Peninsula Republic, perhaps from a country that had formerly been Vietnam or Cambodia. A quiet, introverted woman, she found little time for humor and frivolity. Her body was lean and athletic and beneath her calm and disciplined exterior was the excitement and enthusiasm of energetic youth. Like their scientist passengers, Lieutenant Soo was brilliant in several fields, holding degrees in Laser Spectroscopy, Microbial Mechanics and Spectrochemical Analysis. Her I.Q. level far-exceeded persons four and five times her age. This was not by random chance, but as the result of careful selective breeding and genetic filtering. She was intelligent, but in the captain's mind only a child – wholly inexperienced in life, still filled with wonder at the unending possibilities that lay before her. Though this was the science officer's first space mission, her excitement remained only partially-concealed, inspiring VanDeese to recall a time in his own past when he was just as high-spirited and enthusiastic about the future. That time seemed to him more than a century ago.

The captain didn't know exactly why he and Li Soo wore their standard starship issue uniforms for this mission as they were the only two officers aboard.

Doctor Yale always dressed in her typical medical physicain attire of mint green scrubs under a white lab coat. Mister Saint was a civilian, donning his familiar navy blue jump suit. He glanced at his first officer, the nineteen-year-old female lieutenant looking smart and capable in her matching powder blue uniform. Still, he mused, a certain amount of military protocol was essential for maintaining discipline and rank. Also her choice of clingy form-fitting fabric had a certain way of outlining her lean girlish figure quite nicely.

VanDeese crossed to his command chair in the upper center of the room and sat down. He touched a button on the left armrest and his voice was simultaneously transmitted to the *sponder* implants in all personnel. "This is the captain," he stated. "We are now nearing the asteroid belt. Please secure all equipment and supplies, as we may be making some sudden movements. Secure yourselves as well, to avoid any unnecessary injuries. You will be notified as soon as the ship is clear."

The Chief Engineer sat at his command station on the captain's right. Ron was responsible for keeping the ship's engines and shields functioning properly, and to scan for any anomalies in their performances. "Mister Saint," the captain said, strapping himself in to the command chair's waist and shoulder harnesses. "What size asteroids can our shields deflect without sustaining any physical damage to the outer hull?"

The engineer tapped a couple buttons on a keypad. "If we redirect 70 percent of the engine's power to the navigational shields, we will still have enough inductive propulsion for one-half maneuvering thrust." He looked up from his console to the captain. "She can handle stationary objects up to fifteen meters in diameter, but if they're moving too fast, we may take a beating."

VanDeese pressed a button on the right arm of his chair and a handgrip swung up and locked into position. It was like the joystick for flying a craft in a computer simulation. The main difference was that if he lost this game it would be all over and he couldn't hit 'reset' and start again. He pressed another button on the left armrest and a three-dimensional holographic projection illuminated just forward and left of his command seat. The hologram was a laser-generated cube nearly a meter in size, showing the position of the ship in respect to the moving asteroids. It was a computer composite of the ship's sensor readings, displaying the small hidden asteroids behind the larger ones by using sensor reflection and positional conjecture. *Hypatia* was displayed as a tiny red pyramid about the size of a common housefly, while the asteroids were shown as green wire-mesh spheres, some as large as the captain's fist. The forward view screen allowed Captain VanDeese a better view of the asteroids in respect to his depth perception, but did not allow for side views, nor above or below. Navigation would require continually shifting his attention between the forward screen and the holographic cube.

"Lieutenant Soo," VanDeese commanded to his left. "Locate all personnel and verify that they are moving to the internal areas away from any perimeter quarters, and instruct any stragglers to please move aft and center."

"Aye, sir."

The captain studied the forward view screen a moment, forming a course of attack in his mind. "Well, gang," he breathed. "This is it. Wish us luck." He gripped the steering handle in his right hand and eased it forward, moving the ship into the path of the floating rocks. The asteroids were moving across their path from the same general direction, though their angles and speeds varied. This was probably due to the rocks constantly colliding with one another, or being struck by space debris such as meteors or comets. Some of the floating boulders were immense, most likely the fragmented chunks of a planet or planets and these drifting pieces were all that remained.

VanDeese began to maneuver *Hypatia* into the asteroid belt. Lieutenant Soo called out sharply on the captain's left. "Object bearing two-four-seven, azimuth minus five-four-point-three."

"I see it," VanDeese responded calmly, glancing at the hologram by his left hand. Two buttons by his fingertips on the left armrest caused the ship to raise or lower on a vertical axis. He pressed the button by his left index finger and *Hypatia* began to descend.

The moving asteroid careened into the upper rear section of the city. The bridge shuddered and tilted as the boulder glanced along the side of the hull, deflected by *Hypatia's* navigational shields. The ship rocked to one side, like a tiny boat tossed over the crest of a rolling wave.

"Careful," the engineer assured soberly. "*Hypatia* was designed for transport, not defense."

"This is definitely no shuttle-run," VanDeese grumbled under his breath. He missed the luxury of peripheral vision using his own eyes rather than relying upon a small computer-generated holographic cube for navigation. The captain felt the vibrations under his feet as another asteroid bounced off the city's foundation.

"Negligible damage," Soo reassured without looking up from her science console. "Only a scratch."

"Shields holding," *The Saint* calmly affirmed. VanDeese dared not remove his hands from the controls to wipe away the perspiration forming on his brow. The sounds of the banging rocks became an almost continuous din ranging from the ping and pattering of small, fast-moving rocks to the thundering booms of their more massive relatives.

"Asteroid approaching from three-one-zero, azimuth twenty," Li said. "It's a big one."

The captain shifted his vision from the front screen to the holographic projection. He made a mental note to have a meeting with her later regarding her flair for understatement. This rock wasn't just big, it was gigantic. The boulder was almost half the diameter of Earth's moon and coming at them fast. It would crush *Hypatia* like a gnat without even deviating from its course.

"Twenty-seven kilometers and closing."

"Hold on everyone!" VanDeese ordered. He pulled the joystick toward himself and the ship instantly reversed its course.

" – Twenty-one kilometers – "

"*C'mon, c'mon,*" he chanted as a mantra, willing the ship to go faster. Though there was no atmospheric drag upon the outside of the ship to slow their movements, the engines could only do so much.

Especially since most of its power was redirected to the shields for their protection.

" – Nineteen – "

"We need more speed," the captain cursed. "Mister Saint, reroute all shield power to thruster control."

"John, I have to tell you that we'll be completely vulnerable if we slam into anything."

" – Sixteen kilometers – "

"*Do it!*"

The Saint tapped a few buttons on his control panel and the ship suddenly lurched backwards with surprising speed. VanDeese had to plant his feet firmly on the floor and grip the arm of the chair tightly to keep from shifting forward, the restraining harness holding him from slipping completely from his seat onto the floor. The others held tightly to their shaking consoles, struggling to maintain their balance.

" – Eleven kilometers – "

The ship was vibrating violently, the floor and panels bucking rebelliously. VanDeese gritted his teeth and dug his fingernails into the chair's armrest. The massive asteroid filled the entire forward view screen.

" – Four kilometers – "

"*Brace for impact!*" the captain shouted over the clamor.

"We're not gonna make it," Ron cursed under his breath.

VanDeese suddenly swung the stick to the left and pressed the vertical descent button, throwing the ship into a corkscrew barrel roll. He squeezed his eyes shut and gripped the chair, waiting for the inevitable collision. None came. After a moment, VanDeese opened his eyes and righted the joystick, bringing the ship upright and motionless. All were silent on the bridge as *Hypatia* drifted quietly in space. VanDeese slowly realized that through some miraculous act of God they were all still alive.

"Damage report."

"No serious damage to the ship as yet, sir."

"Mister Saint," the captain said, turning to Ron. "Return power to forward shields."

"You bet."

The captain took a deep breath and eased the stick forward, moving them once more along their course.

"Midpoint," Soo called out, indicating they had reached the halfway mark.

Point of no return . . . Now there's a grim thought.

The ship had rolled and tilted from the bombardments of the asteroids, many sounding like the hammering of giant fists upon the ship's hull. The captain swore at the smaller rocks that were more difficult to sidestep than the larger ones. He mentally compared the experience with trying to cross a busy, crowded room without touching anyone, or they touching him. Except in this case, if they banged into anything, people may die.

The number of drifting rocks passing across the front view screen began to diminish. The ship was nearing the outer edge of the asteroid belt, and VanDeese began to feel a little more confident in his handling of the large craft through the slowly drifting boulders. He smoothly maneuvered the flying city between two immense asteroids, the ship passing through them with only several meters of width to spare.

"Don't get cocky, Johnny-boy," Ron cautioned softly.

VanDeese looked down at the holographic cube. It showed only a few floating green mesh spheres. Lieutenant Soo to his left called, "We are now clear of the asteroid belt." The captain drew in, then expelled a long breath of relief. He released his hand from the joystick grip, realizing that his palm was damp with sweat.

"Damage report."

Li Soo slowly shook her head. "Damage is minimal. Only dents and scratches."

VanDeese looked over his shoulder at *The Saint*. "The engines?"

Ron smiled and lovingly caressed his display console. "My baby's doing just fine. Engines performing at maximum capacity."

Captain VanDeese unbuckled his restraints and rose stiffly to his feet stretching his tense muscles. "Lieutenant," he said, turning to Soo. "Lay in a course from our current location, compensating for deviations in our position."

"Aye sir."

He turned to Ron. "Mister Saint, verify any structural damage to estimate the seriousness and amount of repairs required."

"Sure thing."

VanDeese walked to the door and pressed the pad to summon the *tube*. He turned to his science officer. "I'm going down to the reactor room to confirm that none of the bangs and shakes we've encountered had affected its functioning. Li, you have the Conn." When the *tube* arrived, he stepped in, and the door closed silently behind him.

Chapter 4

The large chamber that housed the nuclear reactor had been constructed with extra reinforcement to protect the nuclear core from external radiation or damage. *Hypatia* had taken a battering and pounding on her trip through the asteroid belt, and Captain VanDeese wanted to personally verify that there were no cracks in the casing or coolant leaks. It would be a shame to get so far only to delay deployment of the city for another six months for the reactor to be serviced or replaced. He passed through two security doors before entering the room that housed the reactor. The extra precautionary measures were for the protection of the inhabitants of the city as well as for shielding the nuclear core from any external influences. The walls, floor and ceiling consisted of double layers of lead and concrete keeping any radioactive leaks from escaping the room.

As Captain VanDeese entered the reactor chamber, he immediately felt dwarfed by the immense bulk of the machinery – a form of humbling he always experienced whenever he confronted the great size of the reactor structure. The nuclear reactor had to be large enough to sustain the electrical and electronic processes of the city for an incredibly long time, perhaps centuries. In the event of a system failure, solar panels would be activated as a backup power supply. These panels, however, would only provide enough energy for life support systems and artificial gravity, and the operation of emergency communication equipment to contact a rescue team from Earth.

The console on the right side of the room consisted of an array of buttons, displays, gauges and readouts. VanDeese checked the readout on one panel showing the core efficiency, performance, and temperature falling within acceptable limits and seemed to be functioning properly. All appeared to be well.

VanDeese stood staring up at the quiet Goliath. The reactor was humming softly, running only in standby mode until the city was secured to the surface of the ice-moon. A massive monolith containing unimaginable power, waiting patiently like a captive Greek Titan, eager to be unleashed and express its full potential and strength. *Such marvels of technology*, he reflected. Power for centuries in one room? Space travel by sunlight? Had man really advanced so far, or were these merely toys of simple beings to inflate themselves to dimensions larger than they deserved? After all, man was still man – fearful, petty, and often immoral and corrupt.

He thought that someday, when man had progressed too far, God – if there was a God – would intervene and cause a catastrophe like Sodom and Gomorrah or exterminate humanity in a great cleansing flood. A devastating phenomenon to reduce mankind back to his humble beginnings. A new genesis of an unpretentious race – honest, moral, and pure. He recalled the words of Doctor Garcia only hours before.

I know I'm not playing God, she said.

Armageddon. A cleansing.

Humankind would need an abrupt jolting of consciousness to become elevated to the next level of evolution. Man had tried to force the change upon himself – by himself – and failed. He had created his own Gods, then exterminated whole nations on behalf of his invented Gods. Patricide, matricide, genocide – doing His work *as* God. All to draw himself nearer to, if not in place of the Creator.

Lord, I am not worthy to receive you . . .

A change was needed, but God had to do it.

Let go and Let God –

God had a plan, a reason for being. If only he could be certain –

Only say the word and my soul shall be healed. . .

Captain VanDeese wished, just once, that God would make his presence known so that he might understand that there was a purpose to all of life's chaos.

Thy will be done . . .

The entire room suddenly shook with an incredible jarring shudder. VanDeese was thrown from his feet and flung into the air. He was caught off guard and only had an instant to twist his body around to keep from crushing his skull upon the solid metal bulkhead above him and deflect the blow onto his shoulder. His body bounced like a rag doll against an overhead catwalk and slammed against the opposite wall, his shoulder blades and neck catching most of the impact. Lights flashed and exploded within his head as his body slowly slid down the wall and slumped to the floor.

He heard his father's voice echoing in his ringing ears. "Johnny, have you been fighting with the other boys again?"

"No, Papa."

"Then how do you explain that cut over your eye?"

"I fell." *I fell . . .*

VanDeese crumpled as a fallen puppet on the floor as he struggled to clear his head. His eyes refused to focus, and the room seemed to tilt uphill away from him. "Lieutenant Soo, report!" he called out to the suddenly silent chamber. There was no answer. "Li, answer me!"

The young science officer's voice eventually crept into his ear, her words weak and distant. "Collision with unknown object," she rasped breathlessly. "Ship has suffered massive external damage. Six compartments in section A-3 destroyed."

Blinding flashes of light flared within his head as he struggled to concentrate. "Seal the doors and air-circulation unit vents in those areas immediately." VanDeese was painfully aware that members of his crew may be injured or dying, but he had other concerns for the time being, primarily the survival of the ship. With his mind swimming and the room reeling, he raised onto his hands and knees and began crawling uphill across the tilted floor to the flickering display console. "Mister Saint," he called aloud.

"Yeah, John," the voice came back. He also sounded winded and dazed.

Had everyone been caught off guard? the captain wondered. "How are those shields holding?"

"Shields stabilized at full power. What struck us was huge – eighty meters across at least. Moving pretty fast."

VanDeese raised himself onto his feet with the use of a nearby hand railing. He stood swaying for a moment, trying to clear his blurred vision and fighting to maintain his balance, then stumbled the remaining distance on wobbly legs to the console. When he reached it, he leaned his shoulder on the panel for support, his eyes straining to focus on the readouts. As best as he could determine, all the displays regarding the reactor's status were the same as before the disturbance. *Good thing for the extra reinforcement and protection,* he thought.

"Computer! Is there anybody dead or missing?"

The infuriatingly pleasant female computer voice returned into his ear. "No personnel deceased. No personnel missing."

VanDeese staggered to the sealed double door. He still felt disoriented, but he had to see what was happening on the bridge. The door did not automatically slide open as he approached. The captain pressed the manual override panel beside the door, but it did not budge. "Computer, open door to reactor room," he panted exhausted, leaning his forehead against the cool metal door.

"Unable to comply."

"Unable to . . .? *Why*, by the eyes of Kohlox, *NOT ?!?*"

The gentle female voice was nonplussed. "Safety precaution sequence number one-seven-zero has been initiated."

VanDeese winced with pain and tried to organize his thoughts. "Explain safety precaution sequence number one-seven-zero," he ordered, struggling to contain his mounting frustration and anger.

"Safety precaution number one-seven-zero," the computer voice echoed. "In the event of a hull breach or unconfined explosion within interior of city structure, nuclear reactor chamber shall remain sealed until such time as it has been evaluated safe by authorized personnel."

"Authorized personnel!" he cursed, his blood beginning to boil. "This is Captain Jonathan VanDeese. Security level three one alpha. Security access code WC2414. I authorize you to open these *blasted doors!*" He pounded a fist onto the unyielding barrier.

The computer responded impassively. "Security access override cannot be performed from present location."

Dios, the captain winced. It made sense. Those idiots had programmed the computer so that if the area had been flooded with radiation, any people trapped inside the chamber wouldn't be able to open the doors. VanDeese rolled onto his back and slid down the wall to squat on the floor. A blinding white light was beginning to grow behind his eyes. "Lieutenant Soo," he whispered, his voice sounding as weak as he felt. "Status report."

This time the girl's voice responded almost immediately, with slightly more energy than before. "The six compartments in sector A-3 have been sealed off. Minimal air and equipment loss. Course trajectory recalculated for shift in position. Proceeding at one-half speed pending Chief Engineer's evaluation of system integrity and performance."

VanDeese closed his eyes and took a deep breath. "Good work. We may lose a little time, but we need to know if the engines have been damaged." He rested a moment, literally willing the nearly blinding lights in his head to go away. "By the way," he groaned, "I've suffered some injury and am stuck in the reactor chamber. The computer refuses to listen to me. As of right now, I'm authorizing you to take command of this vessel."

"Aye, sir."

"The safety of our passengers is your first priority. Verify their locations and have them report to Doctor Yale immediately if injured." He took a deep breath and tried to focus his fuzzy mind. "As soon as you can break away, I need you to come down and get me out of here."

"Understood."

Captain VanDeese suddenly felt very tired. He stretched out on the floor and rested his head on his arm. The bright lights behind his eyes slowly began to recede and fade until they were eventually extinguished.

There was darkness, though not like the cold black endless void of beyond the ship. He surmised that he was not dead, for his body still had sensations; his heart throbbing in his ears, chest expanding as air rushed into his lungs. There was also pain – a sure clue that he had not made the transition from his prior dismal existence. His head and neck stung with a stabbing sharpness and his back and shoulders felt numb. In fact, very little of his body was not screaming for attention.

John VanDeese felt himself lying on his back. The blouse of his uniform was gone, the air cool and soft upon his bare chest. He slowly opened his eyes. There were bright lights, but not as harsh as those that had been behind his eyes. He sensed that he was in a different location. *The Infirmary*, he guessed.

Doctor Bettye Yale stepped over to him. She wore a long, white lab coat over the usual blue medical uniform. "You've taken quite a beating, Captain," she said glancing at a hand-held datapad. "Concussion, dislocated shoulder . . ." Doctor Yale was a small, thin woman with straight gray-blonde hair falling well below her shoulders. Her thin lips turned up slightly at the ends, giving her the perpetual smile of a person who has learned the answers to all the wonderful, mysterious secrets of life. A soft-spoken woman, Doctor Yale tended to her duties with a quiet voice and an economy of words and emotion. Patients found Bettye's calm and sensitive personality both friendly and comfortable, and people immediately and instinctively felt at ease in her presence. The doctor's genuine warmth and compassion for others gave her an aura and presence of internal strength and wisdom. Her dark shining eyes were set in a slim, gentle face with a softness and composure that gave no hint of the woman's true age. She could have been forty as easily as seventy.

"Doctor," the captain acknowledged, his throat dry.

"How are you feeling?"

"*Dios*," he coughed. "My head feels like it's going nova." VanDeese closed his eyes again. "How long have I been here?"

"About four hours. I've given you a mild injection for the pain. You should be feeling better very soon. Just don't try to sit up for a little while."

"The others?" the captain groaned.

"Everyone was caught off guard," she answered. "All personnel had to be treated for dizziness, lacerations and bruises. Myself included."

"All personnel?" he frowned. "Anything serious?"

The small woman shrugged. "Not as far as I can tell. But in deep space, you never know what lingering effects may surface later. We still have much to learn about the illnesses and healing process in this region of our solar system. Frontier medicinal practices may not be ready or prepared to handle situations that may arise in this unexplored territory."

VanDeese lay motionless for a moment, his eyes closed as he listened to the thumping of his heart in his ears. "So much for a nice quiet trip to the Red Planet."

"One other thing, captain," Bettye mused, crossing to a panel on the far side of the room. "How are you feeling . . . emotionally I mean?"

The captain cracked his eyes and turned his head to see the woman pretending to check a medical readout on a display panel. "What do you mean?"

"I've noticed you've been depressed lately . . . preoccupied. Is there anything wrong?"

"Nothing you should be concerned about."

"But I am concerned," she said earnestly, crossing back to his side. "The success of this mission depends upon your being clear-headed and focused on the job at hand." She gently rested her hand upon his bare shoulder. "If this is about a woman – "

"What makes you say that?"

"I know all about your medical as well as your personal history," she stated flatly. "Also Mister Saint was in here earlier for his medical examination – "

VanDeese swung his feet over the edge of the table and sat upright. "I'd rather not – " He paused as the whole room began to spin around him. It took a few moments for his head to stop reeling and his stomach to settle.

"And just where do you think you're going?" Bettye scolded.

"I have to get up to the bridge."

"You need rest."

"I *need* to find out what's happened to my *ship*!" he barked, then instantly regretted it. "Sorry."

"I realize that you have responsibilities," Doctor Yale asserted, "but I insist you get some rest as soon as possible. *Doctor's orders.*"

VanDeese stood on wobbly legs and took the top half of his uniform from the shelf. He slowly struggled with his aching body to get his arms and head into it. "I appreciate your concern, doctor, but there's no need – "

Doctor Yale cut him off. "I am sure you are quite aware that technically I can question your abilities and usurp your command of this mission."

VanDeese turned to face her. "What are you saying?"

The petite doctor crossed her arms and scowled menacingly. "I have every right to relieve you of command of this vessel if I so deem that our superior officer – *you* – is physically or mentally unfit to fulfill his responsibilities."

"You wouldn't – "

"I *might* – if you don't follow my orders and get some rest."

VanDeese sighed, conceding to her demands. "Your point is clearly understood and duly noted."

Doctor Yale was right, of course. He was a total wreck – spiritually, mentally and physically. With his fuzzy brain and aching limbs, he was in no condition to command the ship. But there was no way he was going to let her know that. His pride would never allow him to give the good doctor any satisfaction of knowing just how close to a complete breakdown he really was. He gingerly pulled on his boots then stiffly straightened.

"If the pain becomes too great," Bettye observed, "call me and I'll give you another injection."

"I hate needles," John grumbled.

"No problem," she shrugged. "It's just as easy for me to stick you in the butt, which is just about the only place on you that isn't bruised."

The captain stopped. "Have you been peeking at my *butt*?"

Doctor Yale grinned wryly. "Yes, and in my professional medical opinion, you have a terrific tush. That is, as far as men's derrieres are concerned."

"Sounds like a misinterpretation of the Hippocratic Oath to me."

The woman shrugged. "I would be lax in my duties as a physician if I didn't verify that *all* of your body was in perfect condition."

"*Perfect condition*," he grunted. VanDeese attempted to twist around to see his rear for himself, but winced at the pain and thought better of it. "Is there anything else about the rest of my anatomy you discovered while I was unconscious that I should know about?"

Doctor Yale offered an enigmatic smile. "Nothing I need to discuss at this time."

"You're a very naughty woman." He walked unsteadily to the door and pressed the pad to summon the *tube*.

"Get some rest," she warned.

He turned back to face the small stern physician. "Of course, Doctor," he said, managing a weak smile. "You can rest assured that I'll be taking your medical advice at the first opportunity."

Bettye Yale crossed her arms and gave him a skeptical look. "I'll be monitoring you closer than Santa Claus to see if you're naughty or nice."

VanDeese attempted a laugh, but recoiled with the sudden twinge of pain in his head and neck. When the *tube* arrived, he stepped in and gave a weak wave of his hand as the door closed.

Chapter 5

Before arriving on the bridge, VanDeese took several deep breaths to compose himself. It would not look good for the commanding officer to be seen swooning in pain or staggering from dizziness in front of his crew. When the door opened, he straightened a little, squared back his shoulders and stepped onto the bridge. Lieutenant Soo was hunched over her science station, her hair disheveled and she looked exhausted. An ugly purple-yellow bruise and several small lacerations decorated the left side of her forehead at the hairline.

VanDeese quietly walked over and leaned against her computer console. "Hi."

The girl looked up and gave him a wan smile. "Hi." Suddenly she looked much younger than her nineteen years and less composed as a science officer.

"Li," he said gently. "Has Doctor Yale seen that bruise of yours?"

"She was up here about an hour ago," she nodded. "I guess you were still out of it."

The captain looked toward the engineering station. "Ron's down checking the engines?" Soo nodded. VanDeese stepped to his command chair and gingerly sat down. He swiveled his seat to see his science officer. "Tell me what happened."

"I rechecked the sensor logs," she sighed, staring down at the winking lights on her console. "We collided with a large chunk of space debris, primarily composed of ice and methane gas. It apparently also contained some other element that emitted an unusual form of radiation, partially masking itself from our sensors and giving it the appearance of a gaseous cloud. The sensors did not detect it as a solid object and therefore did not trigger an alarm."

"Have you isolated this unknown element?"

"No sir."

"And the radiation?"

"It is a configuration that has not been recorded previously," Soo responded somewhat flustered. She looked up at him. "It is . . . *unknown*."

VanDeese could tell that Li was visibly disturbed by the damaging collision in both the failure to prevent it and now her inability to isolate the anomalous readings. "Doctor Yale," VanDeese called aloud to the room.

"Yes, sir."

"Lieutenant Soo has just informed me that the ship and crew were exposed to some form of radiation at the time of the collision. Re-examine all personnel as soon as possible for any lingering effects." He looked at his science officer. "That means you too, Lieutenant."

"But sir, – "

"*Now* Li."

"I feel fine sir."

"We still have a long way to go and I can't have members of my crew succumbing to some unknown form of radiation sickness. Get yourself checked out by Doctor Yale. I'll watch things up here for a while."

The girl looked down at her hands resting upon the science console and nodded, slowly rising to her feet. As she stepped past the captain's chair, VanDeese reached out and took her elbow. "Li," he asked gently. "That's a nasty bruise you have. Are you going to be all right?"

She stopped and turned to him, smiled weakly and nodded once. "I'm okay. Just . . . a little tired."

The young woman suddenly looked like a frail and hurt little girl and VanDeese felt a mounting guilt and anger toward himself for her injuries. He was the commander of the ship and leader of this mission and therefore felt personally responsible for *Hypatia* and all personnel aboard. If anybody got hurt, it was his fault. VanDeese found it difficult to keep his emotions from interfering with his judgment where Li Soo was concerned. He had developed a great respect and genuine affection for the brilliant young woman and regarded it as his individual failing when she suffered because of his mistakes. "After you've seen the doctor, I want you to get some rest. I have enough concerns without the additional worry over your health. You're too valuable to this mission . . . and to me."

"Really?"

"Yes, really. You kept your head in an extremely tense situation and handled an emergency alone while injured. I'm very impressed . . . and very proud." The little girl smile appeared again and this time VanDeese smiled back. He gently squeezed her arm. "Now go visit Doctor Yale and then to your cabin to lie down. *That's an order.*"

Soo exhaled wearily and brushed a stray strand of dark hair from her face. "Yes, sir. Thank you, sir." She crossed the room and left in the *tube*.

The captain found himself alone on the bridge. He leaned back in his chair and expelled his breath in a long sigh. "This is certainly no shuttle-run," he commented quietly to himself. VanDeese placed his palms flatly together and rested his elbows on the arms of the chair. He leaned his head forward and touched his chin to the tips of his fingers and stared at the forward view screen into the deep inky vastness of space. Though the ship was travelling at an incredible speed, the stars in the darkness appeared fixed and motionless. Once again, VanDeese was reminded of how insignificant he and his personal problems really were. They could have all been crushed to space debris in the asteroid belt and the universe would still continue to evolve, still proceed in the unaltered course programmed in its inception billions of years before he was born. Life ends and life goes on – only the here and now has any significance to an insignificant few. In the universal life span, they were all merely a fleeting twinkling winking of some distant unnamed star.

Out, out, brief candle.

But they were doing something that would affect the lives of future generations. The *Polaris III* project would bring fresh water and new hope to a weary planet.

Hope he thought, and almost laughed at the concept. Ignorant bureaucratic data-crunchers had forced him to place his ship and crew in a hazardous situation, resulting in unnecessary injury and waste. And for what? *Ice*. He shook his head at the absurdity of it all.

Where ignorance is bliss, 'tis folly to be wise.

The captain supposed that was why so few people were involved with his mission – eight thrill-seeking adults and a cargo of unwanted human fetuses. If the ship were crushed to a pulp in the attempt to traverse through the hazardous asteroid belt and everyone on board were killed, it wouldn't be that big a sacrifice. No big loss. He sat motionless for some time, even after the door of the *tube* opened and the ship's engineer stepped onto the bridge.

Ron noticed his friend resting his head on his tented fingers and asked, "Isn't it a little late for praying, Johnny?"

The captain did not take his eyes from the forward screen. "It's never too late for prayer." VanDeese leaned back in his seat. He turned as *The Saint* passed behind him and sat at the engineering console. "What's the good word, Ron?"

The engineer clasped his hands behind his head and stretched. "Well," he began, "I ran a self-diagnostic program on both the propulsion and reactor systems, and they came up clean. Then I maneuvered two of the external surveillance cameras to get a better look at the outside damage. Only three rooms on section A-3 appeared to be caved in, and could probably be repaired after we've landed on Ganymede. Some other walls had been completely ripped away. They'll most likely be written off as a loss if it's too much effort to restore the missing panels."

The captain leaned back in his chair and closed his eyes. He sensed that the pain killer injection was beginning to wear off. The throbbing in his head was returning and he felt a little shaky. VanDeese raised his hands to massage his temples with his fingertips. He was tempted to allow Doctor Yale to give him a session with an Electromagnetic Massager, but that gave only temporary relief and always left him listless and tired. Ron leaned forward in his chair. "You look a little pale, there, Johnny," he said gently. "You ought to go get some rest."

"That's what the doctor said."

The Saint leaned back and crossed his arms. "I'm no doctor, but I know good advice when I hear it. Go down to your room and get some sleep. I'll keep watch of things up here for a little while."

The captain turned and looked at his friend. "How about you? How are you doing?"

"I'm fine. I was checking a circuit bridge under my console when we were hit. Just got the wind knocked out of me. But your science officer, she was standing beside me checking a readout on the panel there. She flew halfway across the room. Lucky she didn't break her neck."

"She's a remarkable girl."

"Remarkably *lucky*." Ron leaned over his science console. "Seriously, John," he said soberly. "You really look beat. Why not get some rest? I'll call you if I need an executive decision."

After a pause the captain nodded in agreement. "All right. You let me know if something comes up." He stood and walked unsteadily toward the *tube*. As the door slid open, VanDeese turned and looked at the engineer. "Have you seen Doctor Yale?"

"Yes, and she has seen me. A pleasant and rewarding experience for both of us, I must say," he scoffed acidly. VanDeese suppressed a chuckle at the thought of how Ron's derriere might have measured up with the good doctor. Bettye probably knew just how much Ron disliked being examined by persons of the medical profession, giving the older woman a certain gleeful satisfaction in forcing him to comply. "Now, go on," Ron continued, dismissing his commander with a wave of his hand. The captain smiled and entered the *tube*, the door sliding silently behind him.

The *tube* traveled from the boomerang-shaped transport vessel *Hypatia* through the connecting junction on the roof of the city. Though the captain and his crew referred to the entire complex as their ship, technically it was two separate components. *Hypatia* was designed to tow the *Polaris III* complex to Ganymede, then disengage and return to Earth once the Aqua-extraction city was secured to the surface of the ice-moon.

VanDeese occupied one of the rooms of the city's living quarters, but far removed from the others. He enjoyed his privacy and minimized his interaction with the other passengers. There were cabins aboard *Hypatia* for its crew, but with literally hundreds of vacant rooms in the city, he had reluctantly acquiesced. After all, they would have to use the more economical cabins on their return trip, anyway. These accommodations were more spacious and relaxing than the seemingly dark, cramped quarters aboard the carrier ship. The captain guessed that *The Saint* devoted more time and energy to *Hypatia*'s technical and mechanical considerations than to the comfort of her crew. VanDeese really couldn't fault his friend for that. The man was a mechanical engineer at heart, giving little thought of comfort and luxury in the overall layout of his designs. He could sleep comfortably in a conduit crawl space and assumed that others could as well.

The cabin's floor plan consisted of three rooms: a spacious living area and an alcove for the bedroom and a bath. The captain's bedroom held a full-size bed, closet, dresser and side table, while the living room contained two comfortable reclining chairs and sofa, a transparent-topped table about a meter in height, and various shelving for miscellaneous items. It was a sparsely decorated cabin, giving no clue as to the occupant's identity or history. VanDeese kept few mementos and decorations. In fact, he kept very few personal items at all to remind him of his past.

VanDeese staggered into his dark cabin without ordering the room lights on. His head and neck felt numb and his eyes ached. He dropped prone onto the bed and fell instantly asleep. It was a restless, agitated slumber – visions of women's faces circling and spinning around his head. Katarina, Li, Connie, Bettye, Jenny – all demanded his attention, his affection, his desire. "Leave me alone," he groaned, tossing agitatedly atop the bed. He pleaded to be free from them – all of them. Even his beloved Jennifer. He wanted to get even further away from every person in his life, to go even deeper into space and escape every possible living thing. *You're running away* Kat's voice chanted. Yes, he wanted to run away, run from everything and everyone – even from himself.

His long awaited and desperately needed rest was sadly short-lived. After what felt like only a few minutes, the familiar and accursed chirp of the *sponder* implant jolted him awake. "What is it?" he groaned to the darkened room.

Bettye Yale's voice spoke into his ear. "Captain, we've had an incident. Doctor Pollack has attacked another scientist."

"Hal? I don't believe it." Doctor Harold Pollack was a friendly and jovial man and the scientist got along easily with everyone, never speaking an unkind word to anyone. Physical violence was simply not in his nature. "What happened?"

"He was in the cafeteria with two other scientists and apparently just went amok. I have him sedated and under observation."

"And the others?"

"Shelkop and MeGill. Shelkop received a bit of a beating."

The captain glanced at his illuminated wrist chronometer. He had slept for less than two hours and felt he could use about a hundred more. He swung his feet onto the floor and sat up. "All right, doctor," VanDeese surrendered, rubbing a hands over his face. "I'm on my way. Keep everyone there until we find out exactly what happened." He sat and thought for a moment, trying to organize his tired brain. No, it wasn't possible. Hal Pollack didn't have a violent bone in his body. There must have been something to provoke him beyond the limits of his normal patient endurance. Either that or the effects of space travel caused him to totally flip out. VanDeese closed his eyes and shook his head, not wanting to think of that option. If this venture had caused a psychologically and emotionally stable man like Hal to crack up, how could others survive this and other space voyages? What's more, how would the inhabitants of the ice-colony cope? VanDeese struggled to keep himself from leaping to unsubstantiated conclusions. He stood and crossed the room and into the hallway, casting a weary longing look back at the empty bed as the cabin door slid closed upon him.

Chapter 6

The two scientists who had been attacked were still there when VanDeese walked into the Infirmary. One was sitting in a chair with a bandage wrapped around his bare chest. He was the project's hydronics scientist, Doctor Robert Shelkop. He was a lean man of medium height, with fair hair and a faint mustache like peach fuzz. The man gave VanDeese the impression of being cocky and conceited, perhaps from an over-inflated ego stemming from a disproportionate estimate of his own self-importance. Whenever Shelkop spoke, his face took on the countenance of a condescending smirk, as though he were explaining an elementary concept to inferior minds. The captain allowed for such arrogance in the personalities of some of his passengers, for it was their genius and exceptional capabilities that allowed them to participate in this mission. VanDeese found, however, that he did not enjoy the man's company much, and allowed himself few opportunities to spend time in Doctor Shelkop's presence.

The other scientist, Doctor Daniel MeGill, was standing beside him leaning against the wall, his arms crossed. He was a big man bordering on obese with a ruddy complexion below curly red hair and beard. MeGill kept pretty much to himself and was a deep-thinking, studious man specializing primarily in structural mechanics. He said little unless spoken to, more as a result of being introverted than being unfriendly. VanDeese looked them over for a second, then asked Doctor Shelkop, "Are you all right?"

"Just a cracked rib," he answered weakly.

"So what happened?"

"We were just having a bite to eat," Shelkop explained. "We were sitting at a table in the cafeteria discussing hydro-extraction and purification methods. All at once Pollack stopped speaking in mid-sentence and his expression went blank. He just sat there staring at me, looking as though he were in a trance." Shelkop shifted his eyes to his companion, then back to the captain. "His face suddenly contorted with rage. He leaped across the table and attacked me."

"Did you say anything to him that he may have taken as an insult?"

The scientist shook his head. MeGill injected, "We were only discussing new ice-mining theories and comparing them with proven practices. The guy just went berserk for no reason. Ranting like a maniac. Climbed across the table and started beating on Shelkop here. The two were rolling on the floor before I realized what was happening. Luckily I was able to pull them apart, or else Pollack may have strangled this man to death."

"Hal Pollack did this to you?" VanDeese asked skeptically, gesturing to the man's bandaged chest.

"Yep," MeGill nodded.

"The guy went nuts," Shelkop sneered.

"What was Doctor Pollack ranting about?"

Shelkop shrugged. "He was screaming things like *'liar,' 'traitor,' 'thief'. . . .*"

VanDeese studied the two men. "Any idea what he may have meant by that?"

The two scientists exchanged glances. Shelkop looked up at the captain and shook his head. "None whatsoever."

VanDeese scowled at the floor for a moment and sighed. "Thank you for your help and cooperation, gentlemen. I apologize for Hal's strange behavior and will personally see to it that everything is done to discover the cause of his mysterious outburst. If you think of any details you may have overlooked, please let us know." Doctor MeGill nodded and helped the injured man to his feet and they left together. Captain VanDeese walked into the adjoining room of the Infirmary. It was designed for the treatment of patients diagnosed with serious or chronic conditions. He was amazed at all the equipment surrounding him. There was enough medical gear in the room to furnish an entire hospital. Images of Mary Shelley's *Frankenstein* passed through the captain's head.

They have acquired new and almost unlimited powers; they can command the thunders of heaven, mimic the earthquake, and even mock the invisible world with its own shadows.

Connie Garcia's voice echoed once more in his brain – *I know I'm not playing God.*

Doctor Pollack lay stretched out on one of the raised tables. Bettye Yale stood beside his bed, adjusting a plastic bag hanging from a telescoping arm extending from the wall. A thin transparent tube snaked down from the bag, ending in a needle that had been inserted in the patient's left arm. A clear fluid was falling a single drop at a time from the bag into the tube.

The captain stepped quietly over to the bed. The scientist appeared to be asleep. "Why do you have that hose stuck in his arm like that?" Vandeese asked, talking to the physician but speaking at the man.

"I admit it is rather archaic," the doctor mused. "I had to place the patient on a diluted sedative solution introduced intravenously. It was to keep him stabilized while I run my tests without having to subject his system to the trauma of repeated hypospray injections."

"I hate needles," the captain shuddered. "Can't you keep his body in suspended animation, rather than hooked up to tubes like that?"

Bettye Yale shook her head. "If we knew the cause of his outbreak, yes. I don't want to risk an incorrect diagnosis by altering his brain activity or neurological functions."

The captain frowned. "I can't believe Hal started swinging at somebody for no good reason. I was talking with him myself in the city's Botanical section just a short while ago and he seemed perfectly normal. It's hard to accept he would just lose control like that. There has to be a reason. Maybe he hit his head during the collision causing a hallucinatory episode."

Bettye Yale shook her head and turned toward her desk. "I checked everyone thoroughly – "

"Some more thorough than others."

She awkwardly cleared her throat and glanced at the datapad in her palm. "I checked everyone after the accident and found no evidence of cerebral trauma in Doctor Pollack."

"The radiation maybe?"

"Perhaps."

"Perhaps isn't good enough," he scowled, leaning over the bed at the thin woman. "I have a hunch it has something to do with the collision and exposure to that asteroid's radiation. If there's something about that asteroid that could be affecting my crew and passengers – "

"It's too early to tell anything. The tests I've run so far have proven inconclusive."

"Then perhaps you would care to speculate?"

The doctor crossed to her desk and dropped frustrated into the chair. She leaned back and closed her eyes. "At first glance, my thoughts were toward Space Isolation Syndrome." She rubbed her eyelids with the tips of her slim fingers. "It's like claustrophobia. Paranoia and delusional perceptions brought on by the sudden awareness of captivity and isolation. It's when the patient realizes he is no longer a part of the Earth, no solid foundation beneath his feet, no sky overhead."

The captain turned toward her. "But you don't think this is the case."

She opened her eyes and looked at him. "The outburst came on much too sudden, and was directed toward a specific person, not his environment." Doctor Yale leaned forward and placed her elbows on the desk. She looked at her clasped hands and shook her head. "I just don't know. I need to run more tests."

VanDeese glanced back at the sleeping scientist then turned to the aged doctor. "I'd like for you to run every test you can think of . . . neurological, chemical, even subatomic molecular analysis. If this man had some kind of hysteria or dementia resulting from radiation exposure, it means we all may be at risk."

"All right," Bettye nodded. "I'll get right on it."

Captain VanDeese turned and headed for the door. He stopped in the open doorway and turned back. "Thank you, Bettye. These last few hours have been rough on all of us. Please inform me when you discover anything. I'll be in my cabin." He smiled at her. "Following doctor's orders."

Doctor Yale returned the smile, and the captain left.

Something kept nagging at the back of his mind. His brain was still foggy and he had to concentrate. *Li.* Yes. He was concerned about the health of his science officer and hoped she hadn't become ill. "Computer," he said aloud as he stood in the corridor just outside the entrance to the *tube*. "Please give me the location of Lieutenant Soo."

"Lieutenant Soo is in her quarters."

"*Good*," he muttered under his breath. "At least she's being reasonable and avoiding the bridge for a little while."

The captain stepped into the *tube*. "Level D," he ordered. "Crews' quarters." The lift deposited him on the level of the crews' cabins and he walked down the corridor to Li Soo's room. Surprisingly, her door did not immediately open for him as he approached. VanDeese stood in the hall waiting for the door to open, occasionally glancing up and down the vacant passageway in either direction, feeling just a little foolish.

What's keeping her? the captain wondered, beginning to get a little worried. Maybe the girl was sick after all. Suddenly it dawned on him that perhaps she may have been sleeping all the while and deactivated the auto-open sensor for privacy. He remembered that he was also trying to catch some shuteye before being summoned to sickbay.

VanDeese turned and started to head back toward the *tube* when the door to Li's cabin suddenly slid open. He paused and looked back through the open doorway, finding the room cast in darkness. *She had been sleeping* he thought. He took a tentative step inside the female officer's cabin. It was completely dark except for the yellow rectangle of light from the hallway framing his shadow upon the carpet. VanDeese glanced around at the gray shadowy forms but saw no movement. He took another step into the room and the door closed silently behind him, plunging him into the darkness.

"Li?" VanDeese questioned, his voice barely above a whisper. The deafening silence and sudden loss of light was somewhat disorienting and made him a little uneasy. He was, after all, in a woman's private sanctum. *Terra incognita.*

In an alcove off to his right, a soft light illuminated as Li's hand touched the base of the lamp on a table by her bed. "Captain?" she yawned, her voice sounding soft and dreamy. "What is it?"

The light was subdued, falling across the young woman's slender body from her shoulders downward, not allowing him to see her face. She lay on top of the bed, apparently wearing nothing but a red silk robe belted at the waist. Her robe stopped just above her knees, exposing smooth tan legs and dainty bare feet. The light accentuated each curve of her body, every mound, every valley. The young teenage officer suddenly looked every inch a woman.

John VanDeese realized that he had been holding his breath. He was instantly grateful that she had not ordered the room lights on, for he felt as though he may also be blushing. He was shamefully aware that he was staring at her body, but he just couldn't force his eyes away from her. She was so beautiful –

"I . . . uh," he stammered. "I just wanted to see you. I mean, to see . . . how you were feeling." *Idiot* he thought. *You're acting like a nervous little schoolboy.*

"I was feeling a little woozy," she admitted dreamily. "It must be an after-effect from hitting my head." Her gentle voice drifted across the darkness like a light wispy vapor filling the distance between them. "I was only going to lie down and rest a while, but I must have dozed off. My head feels much clearer now."

VanDeese watched the sheer fabric draped across her lithe body rise and fall with her breathing. He was now shockingly aware of what a beautiful sensuous woman his young science officer truly was. He had only thought of her as merely a girl, not a woman nearly in her twenties. She was always so serious and proper in his presence. It was hard for VanDeese to believe that this unemotional female was even capable of passions, desires, and love. He had been in such ill temperament these last few weeks that he had hardly given the time of day to the young officer. Oh, he had obviously noticed that the woman was indeed physically attractive, but for the first time in almost a year he began to feel the familiar deep stirrings of strong affection and, surprisingly, even physical desire for a woman. Katarina had tried to force his old passions to resurface and failed. They were waiting dormant for the proper stimulus and Jonathan VanDeese found this young Asian woman quite stimulating indeed. He hoped it wasn't merely the effects of the asteroid's collision and radiation that was causing his mind to generate sensual erotic imagery involving the young female officer. It would be much nicer to have his old suppressed emotions and feelings resurface naturally rather than as a result of a hallucinatory episode.

After a long pause, VanDeese cleared his throat. "Well, now that I've seen you, or at least seen *some of* . . . I mean . . . that isn't to say that I haven't seen *enough* of you already, but judging from what I *have* seen – " *Shut up, stupid and quit while you're behind.*

"You're babbling."

"What?"

"Babbling, sir."

"Am I?"

"Yes."

"Sorry," he mumbled. "I'll, uh . . . I'll leave you to get some rest." He turned toward the door and it instantly slid open, the light of the corridor nearly blinding him.

As the captain stepped into the doorway, she called to him in a gentle voice, "John." He stopped and looked in her direction. Li had raised herself slightly, shifting her weight onto one elbow. As she did so, her young breasts moved forward and forced the loose silk robe to gape open wider. The light from the lamp now offered VanDeese a better view of her bare neck and chest. Part of her face was now within the illumination of the lamp, and the captain could see that her dark hair was tousled and mussed. It was quite a change from the normally neat and proper first officer. He smiled, thinking how pleasant it might be to see her in the morning this way.

"Thank you for coming," Li murmured with an undisguised tone of warm affection. "I appreciate your concern." Her voice held the faint suggestion of a smile in it. She casually and absently drew her foot up under her and raised her knee. The red silk robe fell back, offering VanDeese a greater view of her lower body, accentuated with shadows cast from the table lamp.

"*Dios*," he whispered under his breath. She was so very beautiful and he suddenly felt himself becoming sexually aroused. He brought his hands together to cover his crotch and felt immediately grateful that the lights were still dimmed. He hoped that she couldn't see his arousal and come to the wrong conclusion of why he intruded into her cabin. Maybe with the corridor light behind him, his silhouette wouldn't reveal the change in his lower extremities. "I was worried about you. About your health, I mean." The desire to go to her was tremendous, to take her into his arms and kiss her on the lips, on her neck, over her smooth nubile body. "I'd, um . . . like to see more of you. Well . . . not now, I mean, but away from the bridge some time. You know . . . maybe do something together?" He knew he was jabbering on like a fool, but he couldn't let the opportunity slip away, not while he had the courage to speak to her alone like this.

Li Soo leaned forward and her breasts strained against the sheer fabric forcing the robe wider. "Are you asking me on a *date*?"

VanDeese quickly averted his gaze to the floor and shifted his feet awkwardly. "Not really a *date*, *per se* . . ." He looked up at her sweet countenance and sighed. "I'm sorry. This kind of thing is difficult for me. Talking with women I mean. I just thought . . . well, maybe . . ." He lowered his head and sighed dejectedly. "I'm glad you're feeling better." He turned for the door. "I should leave you to get some rest."

"John."

He stopped in the doorway and turned. She had drawn her legs under her and raised up to kneel upon the bed. "I think you're very sweet. Of course I'd like to see you away from the bridge. I was wondering if you'd *ever* ask me. That is, if that's what you're doing. Asking me?"

VanDeese relaxed and let his breath out in a smile. "Well, yes. I guess I am."

Li Soo stretched a hand out to him. "Come here, silly," she giggled.

As he stepped toward her, the door slid shut behind him, casting the room into darkness, except for the dim lamp by her bed. John could only see a bare knee and calf and the lower hem of her silk robe. He cautiously crept the remaining distance, stopping when he felt her small hand softly touch his chest. Her fingers slowly slid up to his neck and then his face. He felt her warm breath as she drew nearer, her lips softly resting upon his. It was not a passionate kiss, but of true warmth and affection, her lips lingering only a moment before withdrawing. "*Mmmm*," she sighed. VanDeese could not see, but knew the girl was smiling. He was smiling, too. He brought his hands up to her face and returned the kiss. "Nice," she cooed. "Very nice."

"Yes."

"I've been wondering about this moment for a long while."

"This moment?"

"Yes."

"A long while?"

"*Mmm hmm*."

"How long?" he whispered.

"Oh . . . since we left space dock."

"That long, eh?"

"*Mmm hmm*."

"For this?" he whispered, bending his face lower and kissing her once more on the lips.

"*Mmm hmm*."

He kept his face near hers, his lips barely brushing hers as he spoke. "You were waiting for that?"

"*Mmm hmm*."

"And wondering?"

"Yes."

He smiled. "Was it worth the wait?"

"*Mmm hmm*."

She raised her face and kissed his lips once more, this time allowing more of her hidden passions to the surface. When she released him, it was his turn to say, "*Mmmm* . . . very nice." He smoothed and caressed her dark hair with his hand. "I'm sorry."

"Sorry?" she whispered. "For what?"

"For not noticing you. For not seeing that you were so – " He let his voice trail away. "I've been a little . . . *distant* lately."

"I guess I'm sorry too," she chuckled in the dark, her hand caressing over his neck and down to his chest. "When I first saw you I thought you were very cute."

"That's nothing to apologize for."

"Not that," she laughed softly. "I wanted to make a good impression. I wanted you to be glad and proud you selected me for this mission. That's why I was a bit distant myself. I wanted my abilities to speak for themselves."

"You're a very capable science officer," he said softly raising his hand to brush away a few strands of silky black hair from the dark bruise on her forehead. "And a terrific kisser."

She pulled his face very close to hers, her lips brushing against his as she spoke. "I've been saving them for the right lips."

"The right lips you say?"

"*Mmm hmm.*"

"And are they?"

"*Mmm* . . . possibly."

"Possibly?"

Li nibbled on the corner of his mouth. "All right . . . *probably*."

"Probably?" He moved his lips along Li's soft cheek to the smooth skin below her ear and heard a short intake of breath as he gently kissed her neck.

"Oh *undoubtedly*," Li gasped.

VanDeese drew back and smiled. "I'll leave you to get some rest," he whispered.

Li raised a hand and caressed his cheek. "That may not be so easy now," she murmured back.

"We still have a mission to complete," he said. "I'll need you healthy and well when we reach Ganymede."

"Aye, captain," she sighed demurely, lying back onto the bed and gazing dreamily up at her commander. "Good night, sir."

Dios, she looked beautiful.

In the hallway, the captain pressed the pad to summon the *tube* and the door slid open immediately. He didn't step inside, but lingered a few moments to compose himself and allow his breathing, pulse, and other parts of his anatomy to relax and return to normal. How could this young girl stimulate him so greatly with just a look and a kiss? Such simple things and yet he remained unaffected by the sultry temptress who tried everything in her power to seduce him?

Perhaps VanDeese had rediscovered that missing component – that single element which gives validity to affection and intimacy.

Love.

Chapter 7

The soft whooshing of air was the only hint of movement as the *tube* quietly transported VanDeese to the bridge. He wanted to personally verify that everything was back on line and functioning properly. The captain suddenly realized that he no longer felt the least bit tired, and that the pain in his neck and head was gone. Actually, he felt pretty good.

He entered the bridge and was relieved to see *The Saint* at the engineering console. "Hey, Ron!" the captain called cheerfully. "How's your sweet *Hypatia* performing?"

Ron lifted his eyes with a curious look. "Nary a twitch," he responded skeptically. "She's performing as well as ever."

"Excellent!" the captain exclaimed, clapping his hands together. VanDeese moved to the science officer's station. He pressed a few buttons by a display screen and brought up a projection of the ship's trajectory and estimated time of arrival. "Computer," he spoke aloud, "increase speed to eight-point-two-five. Adjust navigational shields to compensate for increased velocity."

"Adjustments registered and initiated," the disembodied computer voice confirmed.

He stepped down to his command chair, but stopped abruptly when he caught *The Saint* leaning back with his arms folded across his chest, eyeing him quizzically. VanDeese spread his hands and raised his eyebrows in surprise. "What?"

"All right, out with it," Ron demanded, wagging a finger at his commander. "What have you been up to?"

The captain placed a hand on his chest and replied in a tone of mock innocence, "Why, what ever do you mean?"

"Don't give me that," the engineer scolded. "A couple of hours ago you were dragging yourself around like death warmed over. Now you act as though you could win a ten-kilometer marathon."

"Is it a crime to be in a good mood?"

"For anyone else, no . . . but for you, it's almost a personality disorder."

"You slay me with your cynicism."

"I know you too well to allow drastic mood changes to go unnoticed."

"I just feel good, that's all."

"*Too* good," Ron replied skeptically. "In fact, it's been a long, long time since I've seen you act this comfortable and relaxed. It's almost as if – " Ron's eyes grew wide and he leaned back in his chair. "*A–haaa . . . !*"

The captain sat in his chair and swiveled to see his friend. "What '*A–haaa*'?"

A big grin appeared on the engineer's face. "You can't fool me. You sly dog, you were going to keep this a secret, weren't you?"

"I have no idea what you're talking about."

"You've been getting a little more than *familiar* with our female passengers! Am I right?" He leaned forward, excitedly rubbing his hands together. "I'll want to hear all the juicy details. C'mon, you can tell me. I bet it's your friend Connie . . . Doctor Garcia. Am I right?"

The captain crossed his arms and narrowed his eyes into a scowl. "How can a grown man become so depraved – "

"It's those big, maternal types, yeah!" Ron continued gleefully. "That's it. Captain Johnny playing doctor with the doctor."

"*Ron* – "

"Swapping a little saliva. Flossing your teeth with her tongue . . ."

"That's disgusting."

"Tippy-toes under the table together . . . rolling in the hay . . . horizontal gymnastics . . ."

VanDeese grimaced. "Mister Saint, you have a vividly graphic, though disturbingly twisted imagination."

"I knew it! I knew it!" the engineer laughed. "She's been giving a little accelerated growth of her *own* to your – "

"*First of all*," VanDeese interrupted, raising his palm. "I am not one to kiss and tell, and secondly, there *are* no juicy details to divulge."

"All right, forget about the details," Ron urged. "Just give me general data, like *the woman's name*, *your secret meeting places*, *preferred positions* . . . you know, the bare essentials."

"I'm just in a good mood, that's all."

"Uh huh."

"The ship's back on track, no one's seriously hurt – I'm a happy guy."

"You always were terrible at lying."

"Suit yourself," the captain shrugged.

Ron turned back to his engineering panel, waving his hand in a dismissing gesture. "You are *such* a prude. I have my *Hypatia* to devote myself to and now you've got a lady of your own. What's wrong with a little pillow gossip between us guys?"

Captain VanDeese raised his eyes to the ceiling and wearily shook his head. He allowed a chuckle to himself. His friend was right. This was the best he had felt in months and it was because of a woman. Of course, he thought he should try to keep his emotions to himself for a while, at least until he discovered if Li shared the same feelings toward him.

VanDeese felt a wave of relief in knowing that the period of mourning for Jennifer was over. He still loved and cherished the memories of his first wife, as he knew he always would. But he also knew that she would have wanted him to continue living his life, even if it meant eventually finding someone else.

Continue with your life . . .

The captain smiled to himself with the acknowledgement that one chapter of his life had ended, and another was just beginning.

His footsteps echoed loudly across the white tile floor of the nearly vacant commissary. The large room was designed to accommodate over a hundred people dining at once, as indeed it would in the near future, but the only person using its facilities at the moment was Consuela Garcia. She was sitting alone at a table, eating from a small plate of cheese and crackers and scribing on her datapad, a portable electronic device with a liquid-crystal display screen. She used a hand-held light pen to jot notes on the screen and compare figures with the ship's main computer.

The captain smiled and strolled over to one of the chairs at her table. "S'cuse me, little lady," he drawled in a cowboy accent he once heard on an old monochrome projection system. "But is this here seat taken?"

"Cheese."

"I beg your pardon?"

Connie looked up at him and smiled. "Cheese," she repeated, holding up a small orange wedge in her fingers. "Cheese is a unique and peculiar substance. It has a long shelf-life, travels well in space, and you can serve it at any zero-gravity party."

VanDeese smiled at her. "I just came down for a cup of coffee, but I think I'll have a bite to eat as long as I'm here." He reached a hand toward the plate for a piece of cheese, but Connie quickly pulled it away, slapping his wrist with her other hand. "Get yourself some real food," she scolded. "You're as thin as a rail."

The captain mockingly gave her a formal military salute, pivoted on one foot and strode to the dispensing area. He waited by the unit while it prepared a dish of mixed vegetables and wild rice.

He took his plate and mug of coffee back to the table and sat across from the doctor. VanDeese studied Connie's face a moment, then commented, "You look like a person with a problem."

Doctor Garcia shook her head and frowned at the datapad. "I just don't understand it," she sighed. "That crash we had with that big space-rock must have thrown some of my equipment out of calibration. I was testing a tissue sample before the collision, and afterwards I found I had varying results on the same samples."

"Any chance you made a mistake?" Connie gave him a withering glance. From anyone else it might have made him feel foolish, but the captain merely shrugged if off. "Just asking." He glanced up to see Lieutenant Soo standing in the doorway. She seemed to be making a quick surveillance of the room, as though trying to spot someone among a crowd of faces. The science officer was once again dressed in her form-fitting powder blue uniform, her ebony hair combed straight back with a single silver clasp gathering it at the neckline. VanDeese remembered seeing her dressed in this manner on numerous occasions but somehow this time she looked absolutely radiant. *Easy boy* the captain cautioned. *Get a hold of yourself.*

Lieutenant Soo walked over to their table and stood behind Connie. "Doctor . . . Captain," she said, nodding to each of them in turn.

"Please join us," Connie offered, looking up.

Li smiled. "I think I'll go get some coffee first." She turned and headed for the dispensing area.

Doctor Garcia raised an eyebrow at the captain. "Is that all you two live on . . . coffee? You're both as thin as a rail." She shook her head and picked up a cracker from her plate. "You both should eat more. It's not healthy to be that thin."

VanDeese smiled and privately wondered if Connie was perhaps just a little bit jealous of the young science officer's lean figure.

Lieutenant Soo returned to the table carrying a cup of coffee and a plate of rice and vegetables. "I couldn't resist," she confessed, setting her dinner and cup at a place beside Doctor Garcia. "It just smelled so good and I didn't realize how hungry I was."

Connie smiled at the captain and lifted her chin triumphantly. VanDeese raised his cup of coffee to her in a silent toast.

They chatted amiably about nothing in particular for a short while, but Connie slowly began to take note of how the captain's attention became almost entirely concentrated upon their young companion. She saw that he was taking less and less notice of her and what she had to say. After a while, Connie cleared her throat and said, "I think I'll be heading back to my department."

"Um . . . yes, sure," VanDeese stammered, sorry that he had been practically ignoring her.

Connie picked up her datapad and patted John on the shoulder. "It's okay, sweetie," she smiled warmly. She glanced at the girl, then back at him. "I see you have other things on your mind." The captain relaxed a bit and looked at her with eyes that spoke *thank you*. Connie sighed, recalling the way he had been mooning over the female officer. "Ah, to be intelligent, beautiful and young," she reflected. "Oh well, two out of three ain't bad!" She wiggled a few fingers at them and left.

The captain hardly touched his plate. Most of his time was spent in rapt attention of the young Asian officer, studying every aspect of her face. She continued eating, chatting on about the Ganymede project and other speculations in the realm of space exploration. VanDeese didn't seem overly attentive or even interested in the topic. He was more occupied with studying her eyebrows, her face, her lips.

He was listening to her voice but not following her words. His mind was filled with his own questions. *Would they be together after returning to Earth, or would they go their separate ways? Would he ever see her again? If he was indeed capable of loving again, could she love him back? Did she realize how beautiful she was? Was she even aware of his attraction to her?* All these and a myriad of other thoughts reeled in his head as he stared at her beautiful face. He was amazed that he could actually be thinking about another woman in that way and not feel guilty. Somehow he knew Jenny would approve of this one, that her memory would not be jaded if he decided to become serious and intimate with Li Soo. He felt he might even be able to love again, to open himself once more to a woman, to give of his heart and soul to a person and become intimate once again.

If only he could know what was going through her mind and heart. Could she possibly love him as much as he felt certain he could –

Lieutenant Soo was explaining the details of a proposed mining project on Mars, when she raised her face and her eyes met his. She stopped speaking in mid-sentence, her fork poised a few centimeters below her mouth. Li sat motionless, staring unseeing into the captain's eyes as if in a trance. VanDeese sensed immediately that something was wrong. *Dios* he thought. *This is exactly the same thing that happened to Hal before he went berserk.*

The girl's lips mouthed the words *Oh my* as she slowly lowered the fork to her plate. Her wide eyes remained steadily riveted to his.

Here it comes the captain thought, bracing himself for the attack.

"You're in *love* with me, aren't you?" Li gaped.

This was not at all what VanDeese expected. In fact, it stunned him more than a physical blow. He tried to swallow, but found his throat dry. "How did you . . . I mean . . . who told . . . what makes you say that?" he stammered, trying to maintain his composure.

"For a moment I actually *saw* with perfect clarity exactly what you were thinking," she explained robotically, her voice distant and detached. "I could even *feel* your thoughts. My mind was somehow linked with yours, and I was able to share the images that were passing though your brain." She blinked several times, her mind returning to the present. "Is it true? Was that what was going through your mind?"

Captain VanDeese ignored her question, his mind racing with other thoughts. He had forgotten Soo's initial accusation and was focusing on her later statements. Agreed, it was a long shot, but it all added up and made perfect sense. Hal Pollack had actually *read the thoughts* in the mind of Doctor Shelkop and had discovered a dark secret that enraged him to the point of physical violence.

The asteroid – the radiation – the attack. It all made perfect sense.

The captain grabbed the young woman's wrist and stood, pulling her to her feet. He quickly led her across the room to the door, leaving the remnants of their unfinished meals on the table. "Come on," he commanded. "We're going to visit Doctor Yale." He ushered the startled girl into the *tube* and ordered it to the Infirmary.

As they stood side by side facing the door waiting for the *tube* to deposit them at their destination, Li Soo turned and asked in a soft and gentle voice, "John, . . . do you think I'm sick or something or are you . . . do you . . . well . . . you know?"

VanDeese looked over at Li and saw her staring at him doubtfully, a worried expression on her face. He found he was still holding the girl's wrist and felt her body begin to shake. "No," he stated coolly, easing his grip slightly. He cleared his throat, straightened a little and stared at the door. Then he added softly, almost as if to himself, "You are certainly not . . . *ill*."

"You mean you're really – ?"

"We have a few possibilities we have to discuss with Doctor Yale," he said, avoiding the question. After a moment, he felt Li Soo was no longer shivering. He glanced at her and saw her smiling up at him. It was the kind of smile one expresses when knowing a private secret, and yet it also conveyed gentle warmth and acceptance.

Chapter 8

The figures on the datapad were no help. Bettye Yale sighed and leaned back in her chair, rubbing her eyes. She was tired, so very tired. The strange case of Hal Pollack kept nagging at her, the solution as evasive as sleep had become. She hated mysteries, especially where her patients were concerned.

She leaned forward and placed her elbows on the desk and cradled her chin in her hands. She needed to concentrate but her exhausted mind wouldn't cooperate. Just then, VanDeese strode purposefully into her office followed closely by Lieutenant Soo. "Doctor," the captain said sternly. "Have you come any closer to formulating a hypothesis about Hal's sudden irrational behavior?"

"Not yet," the physician sighed wearily. "And I'm quickly running out of options. I'm beginning to think he just had some sort of nervous breakdown."

The captain assumed a stiff military stance before the doctor's desk, his feet apart and hands clasped behind his back. "I believe I have a theory."

Doctor Yale brushed the datapad to the side of her desk and looked up at him. "Let's hear it."

"I am almost certain that the collision with the asteroid has somehow given Doctor Pollack the ability to read minds." The captain's body was rigid, his face impassive.

Bettye leaned back in her chair and smiled condescendingly at him, trying to suppress a laugh. "I hadn't thought about the ESP factor entering into the equation."

The captain was unmoved. "I maintain this assumption," he continued, acknowledging the science officer standing at his side with a fractional nod of his head. "Because Lieutenant Soo has just now exhibited the same ability." He heard the young woman take in a quick breath and inwardly winced at the realization that he just inadvertently answered her last question.

Doctor Yale shifted her gaze between the two visitors. Incredulous, she implored, "You're *serious*?" Lieutenant Soo crossed her arms and nodded, a wry smile forming upon her lips.

VanDeese glanced at the prone body resting in the adjoining room. "Doctor Shelkop may have even acquired this ability, injecting his own thoughts into Hal's mind."

Doctor Yale closed her eyes and pinched the bridge of her nose. "This isn't happening," she sighed.

"Li and I have just come from the Commissary," the captain explained pacing the room. "She just demonstrated her newfound ability by – " He stopped and glanced over at the young science officer. She raised one eyebrow, wondering how he was going to dig himself out of the crater he was forming. VanDeese inwardly shrugged and turned back to Doctor Yale. "By actually reading the thoughts that were passing through my mind." He knew that the suspected forthcoming confrontation between Li and himself was now becoming a certainty.

"I see," Bettye frowned. "Go on."

"Let's go under the assumption that Doctor Pollack developed this same ability to read the others' minds.

Hal may have discovered something *within* Doctor Shelkop's mind that inflamed him enough to physical violence and therefore attacked him."

The woman doctor placed her palms on the desktop and stared at her hands for a moment. She slowly rose to her feet and walked around to the front of her desk, shaking her head in disbelief. "This is too fantastic." Doctor Yale rested a hip on the edge of her desk and thought for a moment. "You actually believe that something within that asteroid . . . the unknown radiation perhaps . . . has somehow affected these people?"

"You said that everyone experienced a wave of dizziness after the collision," the captain replied. "Yourself included."

Bettye Yale stared at the floor and shook her head. "The neurological tests and brain-wave examinations on Doctor Pollack showed no anomalies or discrepancies."

"Any chemical imbalance or variation?"

"None."

VanDeese frowned. "I'd like for you to rerun your tests on all the personnel again. Search for any data that conflicts with the results of the physical examinations we were all given before we left space dock. Li will remain here to assist you."

Bettye Yale looked at Lieutenant Soo. "You also believe this theory?"

Li shrugged. "It has its merits, and explains Doctor Pollack's strange behavior." She turned to the captain. "But as for me reading your mind," she smirked. "I suppose I'll just have to take your word for it."

VanDeese winced at the barb. "Let's still not rule out possible spells of hallucinatory dementia," he countered. *Touché.*

Doctor Yale nodded and walked over to a side table, picking up a small metal instrument. "All right," she said, turning back toward the captain. "Hold out your hand."

VanDeese extended his left hand as the doctor stepped toward him. She pressed the device to his index finger and he felt a tiny pinprick. An LED lit up on the small instrument showing it had drawn a drop of his blood.

The captain yelped and put the finger in his mouth. "That's why I don't like to go to doctors," he scowled. He sucked his finger, then removed it from his mouth and inspected the tiny red dot on the tip. "They're always sticking needles in me."

Doctor Yale chuckled and looked over at the giggling young science officer. "Men are such babies," she exclaimed. Lieutenant Soo brought her fingertips to her lips to suppress a laugh.

Captain VanDeese turned for the door. "I think I'll have another talk with Mister Shelkop," he said. "Perhaps he might be willing to shed a little more light upon that outburst by Doctor Pollack." He looked into the adjoining room to see Hal stretched out on an examining table. "Don't take him off the sedative until we've isolated this thing. I may be completely wrong, and if I am, I don't need the additional headache of keeping tabs on a potential homicidal maniac."

The irritatingly complacent computer voice informed Captain VanDeese that the Hydronics scientist could be found in the *Syntax* Fabrication area. *Syntax* was a revolutionary polymer-based compound which, in its liquid state, could be injection-molded into any shape or form. It was as light and manageable as aluminum had been, but in thicknesses of ten centimeters or more had the strength and durability of cast iron. Since it was a polymer, it would never rust or corrode, was an excellent insulator from electrical current and worked well as external protective tiles on spacecraft. More importantly, where the interests of this project were concerned, it could be formed into pipes and tubes for transferring water.

The Syntax Fabrication department was several large bays stocked with all the equipment and materials needed for making the pipes and supports necessary for the aqua-mining process. One large storage room held extruded tubes, some with the inner diameter large enough for a man to crawl through. Beyond that was a room which held all the machinery, dies, molds, and forming equipment. Adjacent to these rooms were the storage chambers housing the large tanks of raw *Syntax* in its liquid form. Several smaller rooms branched from the fabricating area. These were laboratories and offices with computer consoles for Computer Automated Design and system simulations.

The scientist was sitting at a computer running a simulation test of a possible aqua-mining design. "Well, well," Doctor Shelkop smiled, looking up from the computer monitor as VanDeese entered the office. "Captain! What brings you down here?"

VanDeese sat apart from him in a vacant chair. "Oh, just stopped by to see how you're doing. How are those ribs?"

Shelkop swiveled his chair to face the captain. "Still a little tender," he winced. "I'll have to avoid the gymnasium for a few days. Other than that, I'm all right." He eyed VanDeese speculatively. "I somehow feel that's not your main reason for seeing me." He offered the captain a forced smile containing no warmth.

The captain returned the phony smile and quickly glanced down at the scientist's right hand which was gripping the armrest of his chair very tightly. *Either this man is in more pain than he's letting on,* the captain guessed, *or he's hiding something.* VanDeese relaxed a little and leaned back in the chair, feeling he had the advantage. Shelkop was brilliant and conceited but the captain was the better poker player. "I must admit that attack upon you by Doctor Pollack has me baffled," he frowned. "Why would such a mild and gentle person go completely stark-raving mad for no reason, instigating an unprovoked attack?"

"I haven't the slightest idea."

"And why would he use words like *liar* and *thief*?" the captain mused stroking his chin. "I'm sure I could think of a great number of descriptive euphemisms to fit the mood, many of which would be far more offensive."

Shelkop glared. "Like I said, the guy was nuts."

"A possibility." VanDeese casually raised his left hand and studied his fingernails. "I have my own theory about what *actually* happened between you two." He paused for dramatic effect, stealing a glance at the scientist's hand. His knuckles were turning white. "It wasn't a case of space madness or temporary insanity," VanDeese continued. He looked directly into

Doctor Shelkop's face. The man was no longer smiling, apparently struggling to maintain his composure. "As you know, I read the portfolios of all personnel before we left space dock. I found nothing questionable, but that doesn't mean that Doctor Pollack didn't." VanDeese reached over and picked up a scribing light pen from the desk. He fiddled with it absently, contemplating. "Maybe Hal discovered some dark secret of one of his travelling companions, a secret he found so offensive it made him *insane* with anger." The captain looked up and saw that Shelkop was visibly shaken, his eyes darting quickly around the room. "Jump right in if I'm getting warm."

After a moment of hesitation, the scientist blurted, "All right!" He paused a moment, searching for words. "All right. I suppose I ought to confess."

The captain looked serenely at the man, showing neither judgment nor surprise. "Confess? To what?"

Doctor Shelkop stared at his hands folded together in his lap. "When I was in my final year at the University, a friend of mine who worked in the Document Archives obtained a copy of all the final exam answers. At that time I was a better-than-average student, and I would have passed all my classes without cheating. As you may have guessed, the temptation was too great. I used those answers. I cheated on the exams." He looked up to see the captain watching him impassively. "I graduated at the top of my class," Shelkop said. "I received all the best offers, the best projects, the best positions." He straightened in his chair. "I'm basically a good man," he asserted. "That one stupid mistake could ruin me."

"I see," VanDeese yawned, obviously not placated. "Is that all?"

The scientist looked startled. "Isn't that enough?"

The captain stared fixedly at the man. "Somehow I doubt that cheating on a test would be enough incentive for Hal to resort to physical violence. There's more, and I intend to find out what it is."

"You're exerting a lot of effort over a lunchroom brawl."

"Perhaps. But when something is puzzling me, I have to keep digging until I've exhausted every possible explanation. I'm not satisfied until every option is explored. After all doctor, until we reach Ganymede I've got *plenty* of time on my hands."

As the captain rose to his feet and turned to leave, Doctor Shelkop quickly injected, "I suppose you'll be notifying the authorities about this."

VanDeese looked down at the scientist. "My objective is to deliver this station along with all its personnel to Ganymede. I have *not* been retained to be your baby-sitter *or* your conscience. As far as I'm concerned, the past is the past. You're obviously a very proficient Hydronics expert or else you wouldn't be here. But the safety of my crew and of this ship is my first priority. If I believe there is any threat, real or imagined, I *will* exercise my position of command." The captain turned at the doorway. "Oh, by the way," he added. "We'll be reviving Doctor Pollack as soon as we've established that he is no longer a danger to others or to himself. Then we'll have his explanation to confirm or refute your story. Good day, Doctor."

Chapter 9

The captain stood in the hallway and pressed the panel to summon the *tube*. The door slid open immediately and he stepped inside. "Mister Saint," he announced to the enclosed room.

"Hast thou summoned me, most enigmatic leader?" returned the voice in his ear.

"I'm going to be with Bettye Yale for a short while, in her office."

"Oh, *hoo* . . .!" came *The Saint*'s voice. "The doctor, eh?"

The captain cut him off. "Don't even *think* about it."

"Spoil sport."

"All right, indulge in your lurid fantasies if you like."

"It's *your* fantasies I'm interested in. Come on, feed my deprived psyche."

"Depraved is more like it."

"All depends on how steamy the details are."

"There are no steamy details."

"Perhaps not to you."

"Goodbye, Ron."

"Party-poop."

The captain smiled and shook his head. He leaned against the wall of the *tube* and took in a deep breath, suddenly realizing how exhausted he was and remembering that he was about to get some much needed sleep when this whole incident began. He was now beyond the point of being sleepy, and hoped to get his second wind to combat the growing fatigue.

Be careful what you ask for, he thought, recalling his original decision to accept this command. *You might get it.*

He remembered why he agreed to this mission – to get away from everything, to literally distance himself from his problems. Nature as well as despondency abhors a vacuum, giving new problems the chance to fill the void. Sometimes trouble and bad luck just seemed to follow a man.

The shuttle-runs to Earth's moon-base were always quiet and uneventful. Much too uneventful. VanDeese felt more like a barge-skipper than a starship commander. The *Polaris III* project offered him the chance to regain some of his former confidence in himself and his abilities. It gave him a purpose – a reason to exist.

C*ontinue with his life . . .*

Yet VanDeese never had his determination tested in a true emergency before. Oh, he had kept his head in difficult situations, exercising coolness of command in small mishaps such as emergency crash landings, blown airlocks and cargo explosions. Those predicaments were nothing compared to mentally wrestling with the dilemma of either protecting or destroying a new humanoid species, a race which in itself, if his suspicions were correct, would be genetically superior to their Earth counterparts. Also fending off the impassioned advances of one of his more amorous female passengers coupled with pursuing a potential homicidal maniac wasn't helping matters. This was supposed to be a delivery mission –

taking the *Polaris III* Aqua-extraction complex to Ganymede, disengaging the transport vessel and returning to Earth. Simple. Only it was turning out to be much more dangerous than any of them had bargained for.

As he entered the medical office of the infirmary, VanDeese found Lieutenant Soo and Doctor Yale leaning over and studying the readouts of a display screen. "Have anything?" he asked, walking up to the women.

"Yes, Captain," Soo said, straightened and turning to him. "We believe we've found something that may explain this phenomenon." She stepped back, allowing VanDeese to examine the display. The computer screen showed two helical spirals, side by side.

The captain studied the screen for a moment, then shrugged. "What is it?"

Doctor Yale leaned in, pointing with her hand. "These are twisted strands of genetic deoxyribonucleic acid, or human DNA. It's a macromolecule that holds our genetic code, and makes us unique from all other species, as well as from each other. These two DNA samples were taken from Doctor Pollack. This one on the left was taken before we left space dock. The one on the right is from a few hours ago. Look here." She pointed to what looked like one rung of the twisted DNA ladder. "See this polynucleotide triplet? It underwent a molecular transformation after exposure to the asteroid's radiation. We found the same variations in the DNA samples of Li and myself."

The captain looked at the two spiral chains, still bewildered. "What you're saying is everyone underwent a genetic transformation as a result of the collision with the asteroid."

The doctor and science officer exchanged glances. Soo spoke in a quiet voice, her words clinically cold. "It seems everyone but you, sir."

VanDeese straightened and looked at her, then at the aged female doctor. "Explain."

Bettye Yale turned to her desk. "You were the only one who had prolonged isolation in the reactor chamber. Its protective insulation minimized, if not altogether blocked, your radiation exposure."

The captain looked again at the DNA samples on the display screen. "Then everyone who was exposed may, at some time, develop the ability to read minds."

"Perhaps," the doctor said, sitting at her desk. "It may manifest in everyone or only a few. It all depends on the amount and duration of their exposure, along with each individual's metabolic rate." The captain looked to find her smiling at him knowingly. "I've discovered that I also have developed the ability. Li and I have been sharing little . . . *secrets*."

"Secrets?"

"Mostly about you," she admitted. "We each had our own personal details to share."

Out of the corner of his eye, VanDeese caught sight of Li Soo craning her neck to get a better look at the captain's backside. He turned and scowled at his science officer, but she only returned him an apologetic smile and a shrug of her shoulders. The captain sighed and closed his eyes. He pinched the bridge of his nose with two fingers and fractionally shook his head. "Bettye," he said gently. "Please verify your results with Doctor Garcia and have her compare samples of DNA from the embryos to see if they also have been affected." He turned to Lieutenant Soo. "Li, go to the bridge and relieve Mister Saint. I'm sure he could use a little rest." VanDeese stepped toward the door. "As for me," he exhaled with a heavy sigh. "I'm going to catch a few winks of sleep before I think about what to do about this impending crisis."

"Do you actually consider this a genuine *crisis*?" Doctor Yale scoffed.

The captain turned to the two women and nodded soberly. "Four thousand potential mind-readers? Yes, Doctor, I'd say we've got a crisis on our hands."

The door to his cabin slid open as he approached and he was surprised to discover that the lights were already on. They were subdued to a shadowy dimness, casting the room into the orange-yellow glow of a desert sunset. He could barely distinguish a dark shape filling one of the reclining chairs. It was a long, slender, human form. Not sleeping – waiting.

"Good evening, darling." He recognized the deep lusty voice of Katarina Tushala. VanDeese stepped forward and the door closed behind him, casting him among the room's warm ambiance. Her shape began to move and uncoil slowly, stretching her long lithe legs from beneath her. He could see that her sinewy figure was covered in a black satiny dress the length of her body and of the same thin fabric as the outfit he saw her wearing earlier. Tushala's bare feet lowered to the floor, her satiny gown parting in numerous long thin strips up to her waist exposing the lightness of her smooth bare skin beneath.

Not again VanDeese inwardly winced. *I don't have the energy to deal with this.*

Katarina rose very slowly to her feet. "I hope you don't mind my intruding into your quarters unannounced," she leered, her voice a throaty purr. The tall, slender woman took a deliberately exaggerated step forward, narrowing the gap between them. Her sleeveless black gown had numerous vertical peek-a-boo slits down the front and a wide opening from the collar to the small of her back behind. The dress was undoubtedly designed to tease and arouse rather than conceal. VanDeese made a conscious effort to keep his eyes from not drifting away from her face.

"Not at all," the captain replied, trying hard to feign a nonchalant attitude. "I was just a bit surprised, that's all."

She stepped toward him again, the lower section of her dress swaying rhythmically between her legs like reeds of grass in the breeze. "It was very lonely in my cabin all by myself," she pouted. "I couldn't wait any longer for you to come to me." Katarina raised her right hand and softly caressed the captain's cheek. "I don't want to appear to be too anxious, but you see, darling, I am rather pressed for time."

"Oh?"

"In a few more days, you and your crew will be turning back, heading for Earth." Her hand slowly dropped from his cheek onto his shoulder. "I didn't realize just how lonely and distant this outpost would be. Or how few . . . *real* men . . . would be left there to keep me company." She tilted her head back a little, several of the strips covering her bosom parting and offering a nice view of her bare chest beneath.

Dios he thought. *Give me strength.*

"What I'm really saying is," she sighed. "I'd like to give you a little . . . *something* . . . before you leave. It would help to . . . shall we say, satisfy my needs until the next crew comes to offer some . . . *relief*." As she spoke, her hand slowly caressed from his shoulder across his chest, down his abdomen to his waist. Her slender fingers deftly dipped into the waistband of his slacks. VanDeese quickly brought up his left hand and caught her wrist.

"Doctor, please," he pleaded gently.

She gave a seductive smile and leaned closer, the front of her dress touching his uniform. "Call me Kat," she purred. The soft mounds of her chest rubbed enticingly against him.

VanDeese awkwardly cleared his throat. "I really, um . . . I'm flattered," he rasped. "But it's been a long day and I'm very, *very* tired." He was grateful that the lights were down low, for if she also had the 'ability,' at this distance she may be able to detect what naughty scenarios were *really* going through his mind. He would never be able to force the lusty athletic siren to leave until either she was physically satisfied or VanDeese was totally drained or perhaps dead.

She leaned even closer, pressing her warm body tightly against his. Her face was now so close he could feel her warm breath on his cheek. "*You know darling*," she whispered, her lips barely brushing against his. "Excitement *creates* energy."

"Really Doctor . . . *Kat*. It's just been a very long day, and I'm still sore from that asteroid hit."

"Poor baby," she pouted. "Let mommy kiss where it hurts and make it all better."

"I don't think so."

"All right, then," she leered craning her neck up, her lips touching his ear. "You can kiss me where I hurt and make me all better."

VanDeese put his hands on her bare arms and eased her away. "Kat – "

The woman chuckled mirthlessly, resting her hands on her slender hips. "Do I shock you?" she smirked.

"A little."

A laugh emerged from deep in her throat. "You military commander types are such an enigma. Rigid and calculating, never letting your guard down." She raised a finger to trace the outline of his lips. "But just get one of you in bed," she cooed, "and it's always the woman who's in charge." She twitched her eyebrows and slightly shrugged one naked shoulder. "Which is perfectly all right with me." Kat slipped her free arm around his waist, pulling him closer. "You'll find I'm *very* flexible."

The captain slowly reached behind him and took her wrist into his right hand. He brought both of her hands together between them, forcing a small gap between their bodies. Katarina hesitated, then took a single step back. VanDeese released her arms and she slowly, seductively began to smooth the black satiny fabric of her gown down her chest and onto her stomach and hips. "There's only the two of us here, darling. You and me . . . man and woman . . ." She lowered her eyes, her fingers slipping into the slits of her dress. "It's perfectly all right if you're tired. I'll let you get some sleep, if that's what you want. I'll just keep your bed warm with you."

Switching to the coy approach, VanDeese guessed. *Keep the bed warm – I'll bet she will.* "Kat, you're a very sexy woman . . . very desirable, and any other time I might gladly – "

"You're thinking of *her*."

VanDeese stopped short. "Her?"

"Your late wife."

"Oh . . . *her*." John tried not to visibly show his relief thinking she had the gift of sight after all.

"You're running from me again, darling." She raised a finger to her neck and absently began to trace a line along the naked skin bared in a slit down along her cleavage. "You *are* still capable of doing it, I assume? I mean, you haven't suffered from such a traumatic shock over the loss of your dear wife that you can no longer perform, or have since sworn yourself to celibacy – "

"No."

Katarina leered and began to slowly circle VanDeese. "And you're not the type to throw yourself into your work . . . just to forget?"

"You're analyzing me again," the captain sighed.

"Sorry," she whispered. "I just want to get into your mind. Maybe then I can get into your – "

"There's nothing wrong with my mind."

VanDeese felt her arms form around his waist from the rear, then move under the band of his tunic and up and under to caress the hair on his chest. "Nothing wrong with the rest of you, either." Katarina pressed her breasts against his back. "I was in my cabin thinking of you. Thinking of us. I became so . . .

intrigued . . . that I just had to be with you. I had to feel this delicious body of yours."

"Doctor . . . please."

"Is the thought of having sex with me so displeasing to you?"

"Of course not."

She slid her body around his side and under his left arm to face him, all the while keeping her hands under his tunic. "*Kat*, darling," she purred lustily. "Call me *Kat*." She raised the front of his tunic and bent her head down to give a long swath of her tongue across his bare chest. She looked up into his face, her eyes revealing a seductive leer as she pressed her body close and rubbed her breasts through the sheer fabric against his naked skin.

"Kat, I – " John's protest was cut short as she quickly thrust her lips against his, kissing him hungrily and passionately, her tongue pressing against his teeth and forcing its way into his mouth.

VanDeese placed his hands on her bare sides below her ribs to shove her away. Kat gasped and moaned into his mouth as her hands swept down, guiding his hands forward and into the openings on the sides of her dress. "*Ohh, yesss*," she panted into his mouth, her lips moving more hungrily upon his.

The moment VanDeese felt the soft flesh of her lithe body his mind ceased to function. It had been so long since he had possessed such a physically attractive woman in his arms as Katarina Tushala. Too long a time since he had held and caressed a desirable woman, one that obviously had a strong desire for him. Yet for some reason he couldn't activate the mental connection between his brain and his lower body. He wondered why his basic animal passions didn't take over, why he wasn't tearing the sheer flimsy garment from this sensuous woman's body and ravishing her on the carpet right where they stood.

He wondered why he was even wondering.

She drew her mouth back, allowing him to come up for air. "I want you," she moaned.

"I can see that."

"Let your little Kat fill all your desires."

"It's less a matter of desire than . . . ability."

"If that's all that worries you," she leered. "I'll do all the navigating and you just follow along." She ground her lips again onto his once more, but could tell that his body was not responding as she thought it should. "Am I doing something wrong, darling?" she whimpered.

"No, no . . . it's me," he gulped. "I just don't feel as though I'm quite . . . ready."

She stepped back and braced her hands onto his shoulders, her face leering mischievously. "Not a problem," she chuckled. She steered him backwards and pushed his big frame into one of the reclining chairs. Kat straddled her legs over John's hips, the lower part of her dress fanning across his chest as she slowly lowered herself onto his lap. She leaned forward, her breasts pressing against the satiny fabric and nearly slipping out from beneath. "Relax and leave everything to me," she cooed. "I'll have you ready in no time."

"But, it's been a year since – "

Kat leaned down and nuzzled his ear. "SShhhh," she whispered. "It's just like swimming, darling. You never forget how." She raised up and gave VanDeese a devilish grin. "What do you say we take the *plunge*?"

"I . . . appreciate the offer, but . . . "

Katarina threw her head back and laughed out loud. "*Offer*? Darling, I'm practically *raping* you!"

"I can see that."

"Relax, darling, and leave everything to Kat. *Oh*, you've made me so *hot*! My body feels like it's on *fire*."

She began to slowly gyrate her hips, grinding herself onto his lap. He looked down below her breasts to her lower body and even in the dim light could tell she had nothing on beneath the revealing dress. Kat closed her eyes and tilted her head back, her mouth slightly open and her breath coming in slow gasps.

If I don't stop this now he thought, *I'm in for the duration.*

VanDeese raised his hands and clasped her naked sides, pressing her back and forcing her to rise from the chair. The woman's eyes opened wide with a look of surprise and irritation of having been interrupted. "Really Kat, please. This has been a truly exhausting day. Some other time."

Tushala's face was a stony mask of self-control. Clearly she was a woman who did not receive rejection often. Her eyelids dropped slightly, her lips pursed into a faint sardonic smile. "All right," she conceded, taking a step back. She paused for a moment, her fingertips slowly caressing up the sides of her black silky gown and over the breasts scarcely concealed beneath the slitted black fabric. Katarina raised her chin and inclined her body slightly forward, allowing VanDeese one last view of what she had to offer. Under more normal circumstances he might readily and eagerly dive at the opportunity for a little stress alleviation with this willing and able partner, but he was just too exhausted and if he yielded to her advances now there'd be no turning back. The woman straightened her spine as her hands drifted slowly downward, pressing the black satiny fabric to her body as they went. The palms of her hands slid down her abdomen and around her hips, and she turned slightly aside from the captain as her hands caressed down over her thighs and buttocks.

Dios he groaned. *Give me strength.*

Tushala gave VanDeese a dreamy wink of one eye and said, "You really are an awful tease, you know." She took several very slow and deliberately seductive strides to the door. When the door slid open, she raised her arm and rested a hand on the doorframe. The woman turned her head and body in profile, the light of the hallway making her slender body a slinky black silhouette. Katarina wanted to give the captain one more lasting appraisal of her body, and what he would be missing. "If you change your mind," Kat purred in her deep throaty voice. She removed her hand from the doorframe and tapped a spot just behind her earlobe. "Just whistle." She let her finger slowly trace a line from her ear, down along her neck to the cleft between her breasts. The woman gave a flirting smile, batting her dark lashes as she stepped out of the room, the door sliding quietly behind her.

VanDeese stood immobile, staring silently at the closed door for a few moments. He dropped heavily into the chair, spewing out his lungs in a long breath and closing his eyes. "This is *definitely* no shuttle-run," he groaned.

VanDeese lay on his bunk fully clothed. He was too tired to take a shower or undress, though Katarina would have been eager to help with either. The moment his head hit the pillow he fell into a restless, fitful sleep. He dreamed he was in a room surrounded by dark, faceless strangers– all of them reading his thoughts, probing his mind, knowing his secrets.

He felt as though his inner soul had become naked and exposed, that all of his dark secrets had been revealed. All the lies, half-truths and deceptions were known to all. Li and Kat appeared out of the mist stretching their arms out invitingly to him, beckoning VanDeese to come closer. Their faces slowly changed to disappointment and dismay as his true concealed thoughts became clear to them. Both turned sadly away as they realized his unexpressed love and passion for the one and sexual desire for the other. The two women slowly faded into the swirling fog and a vision of Jennifer materialized before him, her hair and body dripping with briny seawater. Her eyes were filled with tears, her body shaking with sobs of torment from the realization of his suppressed anguish and anger over her death.

In his dream VanDeese found himself staring down into his hands, finding them holding a beautiful ornate box containing his secrets, his dreams, his hidden desires. Suddenly the lid blew off in a gust of wind, and all its contents were dispersed. All his dreams and secret longings were flitting and floating away, drifting and scattering like fallen leaves – too far apart to be retrieved, leaving only the empty container as stark and uninviting as a coffin. Perhaps that was all his whole wretched life amounted to – what his soul essentially was – an empty coffin waiting to be filled.

VanDeese awoke and found his body soaked with sweat. He checked his wrist chronometer and discovered that only a little over three hours had passed. He dragged himself out of bed and stripped off his clothes. After he had taken a long hot shower, he trudged back to his bedroom and pulled on a fresh uniform.

Bettye Yale's voice leaped into his ear. "Sorry to disturb you, captain," she said. "But I have some bad news."

What other kind of news is there? he winced. "All right, let's have it."

There was a brief pause. "Hal Pollack is dead."

Chapter 10

Captain VanDeese didn't blame Doctor Yale personally for the accidental death of Hal Pollack. Sure, she was a very competent physician, but with all of those gizmos, gimmicks and electronic gadgetry at her disposal it was no small wonder that more people weren't victims of erroneous medicine. This was merely his own personal preconception regarding the area of medicine in general because of his lifelong loathing of hospitals. Medical science had progressed significantly in the past century, though it was not infallible, as the still-warm corpse of Doctor Pollack confirmed. Bettye Yale was pulling a sheet over the face of the now late Doctor Harold Pollack as the captain entered the Infirmary. "What happened?" he demanded.

Bettye looked at him and frowned. She appeared visibly shaken at having lost one of her patients. "I intended to take him off the sedative when I came back from conferring with Connie Garcia," she explained. "We both confirmed that Hal was neither ill nor insane. Apparently, something about his chemical or metabolic makeup allowed his mind-link ability to develop more rapidly than everyone else. It was his violent outbreak that had us baffled, leading us to believe it was some form of dementia. If we had discovered his ability in some other way he might . . . well, it's purely academic now." She sighed deeply. "I arrived here to discover that someone had tampered with the intravenous line." She walked from the room and the captain followed.

He felt as though they intended to discuss something very private that they didn't want the corpse to overhear. Doctor Yale stopped abruptly and turned. "When I said *tampered*," she stated flatly. "I actually meant that he was *murdered*."

"Murdered?" *Dios – a killer on board. That's all I need.*

"I'm afraid so, yes," she nodded.

VanDeese hesitated, allowing the implications to sink in. *Who would want to kill Hal?* he wondered. True, he didn't know the man very well, but after only a short time in isolation aboard the ship, acquaintances and friendships grew quickly. They were all strangers at the onset of the mission. Yet, what VanDeese knew of Hal, the man didn't have an enemy in the galaxy. He never spoke an unkind word nor used a criticizing tone of voice. He was the most amiable man that the captain had ever met, and yet, somebody killed him – perhaps to disguise a greater crime. Doctor Pollack had to be silenced permanently to avert attention away from the guilty party. But then, that's usually how it worked – the innocent pay for the crimes of the guilty. In a very true sense, Hal was the sacrificial lamb, but to what purpose VanDeese could not even speculate. One thing was for certain – he was going to find out. "How was it done?"

The small woman turned and walked slowly to her desk. As she sat down, the captain could see that she, too, was on the verge of total exhaustion. "I found that the chambers of the heart had a large quantity of air in them. The killer injected an air bubble into the line. It traveled through his veins, and when it reached his heart, it stopped." She looked at her hands clasped atop the desk. "At least it was painless. He didn't suffer."

VanDeese crossed his arms and stared at the doorway to the body beyond. "There's only one person who comes to my mind who had a grudge against Hal. Doctor Shelkop gave me some lame story about his defrauding a college exam, but I'm convinced it goes much deeper and is far more sinister than that."

"Or else somebody wants us to *think* it was him," the doctor added.

The captain slowly paced the doctor's office for a few minutes, pondering the implications and possibilities. Even if Shelkop had murdered Hal, there was no evidence against him. Unless the man confessed to the crime, there was nothing anyone could do. They could obtain the truth from him by using their mind-link – brain-probe – whatever they called it, but it would be inadmissible in court. *Two of my crew sucked the confession right out of his brain, Your Honor.* Yeah, right. Unless VanDeese was willing to resort to frontier law – becoming his own judge, jury and executioner – the killer would go free. They needed evidence or a confession. But how?

He glanced up at a panel on the wall to the left of Bettye's desk. It was a bank of numbers with liquid crystal display readouts below. Some were flashing, others were not. "What is this?" he pointed.

"Those are the data displays from our *sponder* implants."

VanDeese peered closely at the digital readouts. "Which number am I?"

"You're number two," Bettye said. VanDeese turned and eyed her curiously. She smiled and raised a finger. "I'm number one, of course."

The captain motioned to the displays. "Two numbers have no data readouts. Who is number four?"

The doctor's smile vanished. "Hal Pollack."

VanDeese looked back to the display. "And who is number seven?"

Doctor Yale tapped a few numbers into the datapad on her desk. "That would be the stellar cartographer," she nodded. "Katarina Tushala. Her implant must not be transmitting for some reason." She shrugged. "I'll replace it later."

VanDeese thought about Tushala. Could this whole thing have been over a woman? She had made a move on him – not once, but twice. Could she have been the reason for an outbreak among the male passengers? He recalled her statement about how few *real men* would be left when he and his crew turned back to Earth. VanDeese doubted that Kat was behind this whole nightmarish situation. Or was even the cause of it. The words Hal threw at Shelkop – *traitor, liar, thief* – somehow weren't the accusations of a jealous lover. The captain doubted this whole mess was going to be that simple and felt that the death of Doctor Pollack was not going to be the end of it.

Bettye Yale leaned back in her chair. "Connie Garcia was very helpful," she stated. "She was calibrating the cryogenic equipment with a tissue sample when the asteroid struck us. She couldn't understand the data inconsistency."

VanDeese grunted and turned from the display panel. "I recall she was perplexed about it earlier when we met in the commissary."

"She discovered that both readings – before *and* after the asteroid collision were correct."

The captain straightened. "DNA alteration?"

"Exactly," Bettye nodded. "The sample embryo had the same polypeptide variance."

VanDeese resumed pacing in front of her desk. "Then we can assume that all life forms upon this ship have been changed and may possibly gain this new potential."

The doctor nodded. "Connie also verified with me the method in which this 'mind-linking' is possible." VanDeese stopped pacing and stood in quiet attention. "It only works when you make close eye-contact with the subject, one meter or less – distance and mental focus are key factors. The subject has to be thinking of a specific idea, and you simply draw that information out through the optic nerve connection from their brain."

VanDeese nodded with understanding. "Doctor Pollack and Lieutenant Soo were both sitting closely to someone, and mind-link was established when their eyes met."

"Now that we all know what it was Li saw in your mind," Bettye sighed. "I'm curious to know what Shelkop is hiding."

"If you were thinking about a mind-link, forget it," VanDeese scolded. "If he's the one who murdered Hal, the man is too dangerous. He's already killed one person to keep his secret. He might kill again. No . . . we have to think of some other way to prove his guilt or innocence. Maybe somehow we could find a way to play up to his over-inflated ego."

"That shouldn't be too difficult."

VanDeese rubbed his chin. "Even if we *could* mind-link with him – assuming he's the guilty party – we'd have to get him to think about killing Hal in order to draw out the confession." He shook his head. "This mind-reading stuff is getting to be very messy."

Doctor Yale crossed her arms and smiled. "I suppose the old adage still holds true," she chuckled. "The eyes *really are* the windows to the soul."

Chapter 11

"Computer," VanDeese called to the room. "Please specify locations of Mister Saint and Doctor Shelkop."

"Mister Saint is in the Engineering Department. Doctor Shelkop is in his quarters."

The captain turned to Bettye Yale. "I'd like for you to supply me with a tranquilizing hypo."

"Tranquilizer?"

"Yes," VanDeese nodded. "When I find out who's been responsible for causing this chaos aboard my ship, I want him stopped. I need to arm myself and be prepared to act when I find him."

Bettye nodded once, then rose to her feet. As she crossed the room to the pharmaceutical compartment, VanDeese reminded her, "There's a murderer on board this ship. Be careful whom you admit into the Infirmary from now on."

"Shouldn't you arm yourself with something a little more . . . *deadly*?"

"Hopefully, I shouldn't need it," he said. "Besides, there *aren't* any weapons on board." He smiled weakly. "At least the odds will be even."

Doctor Yale returned with a small metallic cylinder, the approximate diameter of a scribing device, but half its length. "Touch this tip to his skin, then press the button on the other end. The hypo-spray should take effect within seconds."

VanDeese accepted the device from her hand and slid it behind his heel inside his boot. He crossed the room to the door. "Seal the infirmary after I leave and take an inventory to see if anything is missing. You have a lot of sharp implements here. The killer may be desperate and dangerous. We're assuming it's Shelkop, but it may be anyone." Bettye scowled at him and he quickly added, "Present company excluded, of course."

The captain stopped in the hall and turned back to the silently closing door. The collision with the asteroid and the subsequent increase in human cerebral faculties may have more dire consequences than he originally perceived. There was the very real possibility that one side effect of this new mind-scan ability was a form of dementia where the person could commit heinous atrocities without any recollection or self-control. He knew that he was exempt, but anyone else aboard could be capable of terrible actions – even murder – with no knowledge of the deed. For all he knew the woman physician herself murdered Hal Pollack with no memory of the crime. An entire race of *Jekyll and Hydes* – the possibility was even too awful for VanDeese to contemplate.

He now had to wrestle with the responsibility of allowing this new race of mind readers to survive. He couldn't permit any of them to ever return to Earth if the DNA alteration made them potential killers. It would be an easy enough task. VanDeese would adjust *Hypatia's* course slightly, then jettison the colony into deep space. They would continue to survive in their floating prison – the reactor supplying energy, gravity and heat. But the thought of losing the only people VanDeese cared about – Connie, Ron, and now Li – was too much for him to bear.

I'm not playing God, Connie said.

The captain closed his eyes and sighed. He prayed for guidance and almost wished that there were only a single psychopath on board.

These are the times that try men's souls.

VanDeese looked to the closed door of the Infirmary and whispered softly, "Sorry, Doctor, but I have to suspect everyone . . . even you."

The Chief Engineer was in his office, leaning back in a chair with his feet up on the desk. He was staring intently into a small piece of mirror in his hand. VanDeese stopped in the doorway and crossed his arms over his chest. "I'm almost afraid to ask," he sighed, "but what are you doing?"

Ron turned his face to his visitor, showing a lopsided grin. "Just trying to see if I'm keeping secrets from myself. HA! HA!" he laughed.

The captain shut his eyes and slowly shook his head. "I take it you heard the news," he groaned.

His friend nodded and set the mirror on his desk. "With so few people on board, news travels faster than a photon in a vacuum." *The Saint* suddenly exclaimed a loud "*OOOHH!*" his eyes growing wide. He quickly swung his feet off the desk onto the floor. "Come over here so I can read all about your love life."

"Forget it."

"Aw, come on! Humor me."

VanDeese smirked. "You find my love life humorous?"

"There's one way to find out! Sit down and let me probe you."

"*Probe* me?"

"Yeah," Ron smiled. "Just us guys, sharing intimate moments . . ."

"Intimate moments are not intended to be shared."

"Then tell me the name of your mystery woman and I'll probe *her*."

"Absolutely not."

The Saint banged his fist on the top of his desk and the computer monitor hopped a few centimeters along with all the assorted desktop debris. "You're going to make me find out the hard way. I'm gonna discover who you're playing patty-cakes with if I have to mind-meld with every person on board!"

"I've got a project for you," VanDeese interrupted, quickly changing the subject.

"What is it?" the engineer asked, leaning back in his chair.

"I'd like for you to construct something that can be used to restrain an adult."

"I was just thinking about something along those very lines for you, Johnny-o."

"Ron, I'm serious."

"You mean like a jail?"

"I was thinking of something a little more confining than that," VanDeese answered.

"A cage?" *The Saint* laughed.

"Exactly."

Ron's eyebrows shot up. "What are we now . . . *space cops*?"

"Ron, there's a potentially dangerous person on board. He murdered Hal. He may be desperate – possibly armed."

"Murdered Hal?"

"In the Infirmary. It may be related to his attack on Shelkop. We have to be prepared if the killer tries to strike again."

"I see," the engineer mused. "Well, I can construct something with bars of *Syntax* in one of the empty storage bays." He thought for a moment, then nodded his head. "Sure. No problem. Once we catch him, then what?"

"I've given that some thought as well," VanDeese allowed. "Doctor Garcia may lend us some of her cryogenic equipment."

The Saint threw up his hands and laughed. "Johnny-boy, this is the best trip we've ever been on! Asteroid crashes . . . sexual shenanigans . . . murder . . . *never* a dull moment!"

"Captain to Doctor Garcia."

"Please, dearie," the woman's voice laughed. "Call me Connie."

VanDeese smiled to himself. "I'd like to speak to you for a few moments, if I may. It's rather urgent." He glanced at his friend then quickly added, "It's business." *The Saint* crossed his arms and rolled his eyes.

"Sure," Connie replied happily. "I'm in my cabin. Come on down."

"Sorry Ron," VanDeese said. "Gotta go."

The engineer frowned. "All business and no pleasure, is that it?"

"I derive my pleasure from thwarting your efforts of trying to pry into my romantic life."

"Romantic life?"

"Or the lack of it."

"I'm sure the mystery surrounding your sex life is far more exciting than the action."

"You need something to occupy your mind," the captain sighed. "Try programming *Hypatia's* main computer to calculate mathematical puzzles. Acceleration of an object in a vacuum or something like that."

Ron shook his head. "It won't be as fun."

The *tube* deposited VanDeese on the level of Doctor Garcia's cabin. He strode down the hallway and the door opened as he approached. "I hope I'm not interrupting anything," he announced, stepping into the woman's room.

Connie Garcia sat on one end of an overstuffed sofa wearing a billowy garment of navy blue and gold. "I was only reading," she said, placing a databook onto the low table in front of her. She patted a cushion next to her. "Come over and sit. Tell me what's on your mind."

VanDeese walked over to the couch, but stood for a moment before sitting, taking a long appraising look around. The room had a distinctly feminine touch. The walls were covered with landscape pictures and delicate tapestries. Artificial floral arrangements decorated several shelves and a knitted-lace covering lay upon the low table by the couch. "Nice place you have here," he observed, sitting beside her.

"Thank you," she chuckled. "But I'm sure you don't need to urgently discuss my decorating abilities."

"Sorry," he shrugged. "But I believe this is the first time I've been in your cabin."

"You were always welcome," she offered with a smile.

"I know," he sighed, leaning back on the sofa. "I suppose I just prefer to meet with women on more neutral territory."

"Does it make you uncomfortable to be alone with me in my rooms?"

"Oh, no," he answered quickly. After a moment, he glanced sideways at her and added, "Well, perhaps a little."

Connie gently patted his knee with her hand. "So that's what you're here to see me about. A little female advice?"

"Female advice?"

"You know," she winked. "How a man should behave around a young lady, things like that."

For a moment VanDeese suspected Doctor Yale of divulging his earlier outburst in her medical quarters. "Young lady?"

"In the commissary."

"Oh," he blushed, somewhat relieved. "Sorry about that."

Connie laid her hand on his shoulder. "You've just been out of circulation for a little while, that's all."

"Eleven months," he nodded. He suddenly snapped his attention to her face. "How do you know about that?"

"I'm with the government!" she laughed. "We know everything!"

VanDeese flushed. "*Now* you tell me."

Connie smiled and leaned back into the cushions. "Take my word for it, that little girl just needs the right man to *distract* her, if you know what I mean."

The captain cleared his throat, anxious to change the subject. "Thanks for the, uh . . . *advice*, but that's not what I came to see you about."

Connie crossed her arms. "So what *is* on your mind, or do I have to – what was the phrase that Bettye used? – give you a *brain-probe* to find out?"

VanDeese managed a genuine smile, but he diverted his face nonetheless. "I'd like for you to explain to me the basic mechanics of Cryobiological Suspension."

Connie laughed. "You're the second person today who's wanted to discuss cryogenics."

VanDeese snapped his head back toward her, trying desperately to keep the anxiety from his voice. "Who was the other person?"

"Why, it was Robert Shelkop," she admitted candidly.

The captain stood and began to pace the room. "I have suddenly found myself in a rather delicate situation," he said somberly. "As a government representative, I'm sure you're aware of the value of discretion." He turned back to her, and she nodded once, her smile gone.

"Would it be possible for you to equip *Hypatia* with a fully-functional Cryogenic Stabilization Unit for a fully-grown adult?"

Doctor Garcia was visibly surprised. "Fully-grown? I believe it can be *done*, but – "

"I'll see to it that my engineer obtains from you the necessary equipment," the captain interrupted.

"Why can't you have Doctor Yale simply sedate the person?" she protested.

VanDeese shook his head in frustration. "The trip back to Earth is a long one. We're talking *weeks*. For a person to be under sedation for that long, well . . . they might not survive."

Connie frowned. "Very risky. May result in autonomic and neurological degradation, possible muscle and tissue injury. I strongly advise against it."

The captain stopped pacing and wheeled on Doctor Garcia. "I'm not asking for your *opinion* in this matter!" he barked.

Connie crossed her arms over her ample bosom and eyed the captain defiantly. "Bettye Yale is an excellent *medical* doctor, but she's no scientist. The operation of cryogenic suspension equipment is extremely involved and complex. It must have continuous monitoring and adjustments. Not something a person can learn overnight."

"You can teach her."

"Even under the most ideal circumstances," Connie continued nonplussed, "suspending an adult human with a fully functioning neural system is risky at best."

"My choices are extremely limited," VanDeese scowled. "Cryogenic suspension is my best option." He took in, then expelled a long breath. "Look, Connie, I need your help. My crew is too small to add the additional work of guard duty to our responsibilities."

Doctor Garcia nodded grimly.

A woman's voice suddenly exploded into the captain's ear. "Captain! This is Doctor Yale!" she shouted. "Do you hear me?"

VanDeese winced and clamped his hand to his ear. "Yes, I hear you. What's wrong?"

"Mister Saint and Doctor Shelkop. Both of their life sign readings just went berserk, and now Mister Saint's readings have become sporadic. I'm afraid something may have happened to him."

"Sorry, Connie," he frowned. "We'll talk about this later." The captain sprinted from Doctor Garcia's quarters. "Bettye, where is Ron now?" he demanded as he slammed his hand onto the summoning pad for the *tube*.

"Let me see," the woman's voice answered. "*Syntax* Fabrication department."

"*Dios*," the captain cursed under his breath. "I hope I'm not too late."

Chapter 12

The door to the *Syntax* Fabrication department slid open revealing only darkness within. "Lights on," VanDeese commanded. Nothing happened. He peered into the black room, but saw no movement.

He took two steps into the darkened room. "Ron?" he called. A large metal wrench careened off the wall just behind his shoulder, barely grazing his head. VanDeese quickly dropped to his knees and crawled for the cover of the nearest table. As he moved, the door slid closed behind him, casting the room into near total darkness. The only illumination was the eerie blue light of two computer monitors and the various colored glows of switches and lighted meters on the wall panels.

The captain's ears strained in the darkness to hear any movement. His military training instantly took over. His senses became sharper than his natural survival instincts.

The mission comes first . . . neutralize the enemy . . .

He silently crept along the floor, feeling for the fallen wrench or any other object he could use as a weapon. VanDeese crawled along the length of the table, his hands probing for anything he could find on its surface or on the floor. He suddenly bumped into a large bulky object.

It was Ron.

VanDeese felt for the man's neck and detected a faint pulse. The engineer was still alive. The captain's eyes were slowly becoming adjusted to the dimness of his surroundings and he could now distinguish a darker patch of blood along his friend's head and face. *The Saint* was still clutching a *Syntax* rod in his right hand, and the captain gently pried it free. It was about a meter in length and ten centimeters in diameter. VanDeese now had a weapon.

Cry "havoc," and let slip the dogs of war . . .

Defend . . . disable . . . destroy . . .

The captain slowly raised himself to a crouching position and peered over the top of the table. His eyes detected no movement, but after a few moments he heard the thud of someone bumping into furniture in the adjoining room. Someone was in the *Syntax* fabrication area. VanDeese edged himself along the wall to the doorway, both hands holding the solid baton close to his chest. There was no light in the adjoining room. *At least the odds would be even.* He needed to pinpoint the enemy's location before formulating a plan of attack.

"Doctor," the captain called into the open doorway.

"Oh, hello, captain," Robert Shelkop replied in a slow, menacing sneer. "Sorry about the lights. I appear to be having something of a *vision* problem lately."

His escalated adrenaline level made the captain's body as tense as a tightly wound spring, ready to pounce or defend in an instant. "My engineer is hurt. Let me get him out of here."

"Sorry, captain. No can do. He knows too much, and now, so do you."

"Knows too much?"

Shelkop sneered. "Don't toy with me, captain."

"And Hal?"

"You were right about him learning my secret. Who would have known we would all develop the ability to read minds? A pity about him, though. Seemed like a nice enough fellow. Unfortunately he would have made things difficult for me if he had been able to talk. I never intended to hurt anyone, but, *Que sera, sera*."

"Let's talk about this," VanDeese spoke into the darkened room. He heard a drawer open and close. *The man's looking for something*, he surmised.

"Come now, Captain, haven't you heard?" the scientist jeered mockingly. "There isn't any need to talk anymore. All we have to do is look at each other and all of our inner thoughts shall be revealed." Another cabinet was heard opening, hands rummaging in the darkness. "Unfortunately, it's hard to keep secrets that way," he continued. "That botanist, your engineer, even that silly, skinny, stargazing slip of a woman. None of them could keep a secret."

The captain stiffened, his palms sweaty. "Katarina?" he rasped, trying to fight the panic from his voice. "What have you done with her?"

"A funny thing about her," the voice answered matter-of-factly. "She, like that plant-boy Pollack, accidentally read my plans in my mind. Oh, no – not the original plan – the new one. Pollack found out the old one and had to be shut up. I knew you wouldn't be naive enough to buy that stupid story about stealing test answers, so I needed more time." He chuckled to himself. "I couldn't believe how easy it was. I even thought about making it look like an accident but was in a hurry. It was too simple. One little bubble and it was all over." The darkness fell silent for a moment.

"You know," Shelkop continued, "I should have gone into forensic medicine. Human death is really *very* fascinating."

This guy is completely insane.

"Then that stupid Tushala discovered my new plan and I had to dispose of her as well."

"What have you done with her?" VanDeese tried to keep his voice even, but his body was shaking with adrenaline and bottled rage.

The scientist laughed softly to himself. "She came to me seeking sexual comfort. She was *very* persistent – what could I say? Sadly she read my plans in my eyes and had to be eliminated. I had to . . . *persuade* her . . . to take a very long walk out of a very short airlock." He suddenly burst into a fit of high-pitched hysterical laughter, the maniacal laugh of the criminally insane. "She should have thanked me," he cackled. "I gave her the opportunity to get closer and feel more in touch with her work."

This lunatic's completely mad, the captain thought. He crouched low and looked through the doorway. He could just make out the long rows of extruded *Syntax* tubes along the left side of the room. VanDeese thought he might be able to get around them and sneak up on the man from the rear. *Just keep him talking,* he thought.

"So what is this new plan?" the captain called through the door, then quickly sprinted through the opening to the cover of the tubes to his left.

"Plan?" Shelkop wondered. "Oh, yes. Well . . . the first plan – the old one – wasn't mine at all. As you know, the government regulates and has controlling interest in the world's water reclamation and purification processes. That's why this operation was organized by numerous individual private firms, all with common interests. They formed a consortium for this endeavor to increase the amount of freshwater for Earth."

As the man talked, the captain edged silently along the rows of pipes and tubes. He took slow, cautious steps, careful not to make any sounds.

"After this station becomes functional and the ice extraction begins," Shelkop continued, "the privately-held corporations on Earth would systematically destroy or contaminate the output of the government-controlled water facilities. This station would soon become the primary source of water for the whole planet." He paused for a moment. "A silly plan, actually. All the fools were interested in was economic dominance and political control."

VanDeese was now at the end of the row of pipes. The scientist continued to search in the drawers and cabinets. "When we were hit by that asteroid, everything changed. We changed, humanity changed, and my destiny changed. That was when I developed the basis of my new plan, a truly excellent plan if I do say. Think of it, an army of mind-readers, raised and trained to follow *my* every command. Four thousand people without identities who could slip unnoticed into government buildings, business offices, military installations. They could probe the minds and draw out the secrets of any person I wanted. Now that's *real* power."

Doctor Shelkop stopped rummaging through the drawers and cupboards. The captain heard the scratching of metal, then saw a tiny spark leap from a metallic flint-igniter. The blue-wedge flame of a hand-held propane torch used for cutting irregular-shaped holes into the extruded *Syntax* pipes illuminated the darkness.

"Of course, you and your crew will have to go," the scientist sighed. "The authorities will receive my message that you all died from radiation exposure from that asteroid. I'm sure I can find a way to make the computer establish a stationary orbit around our little ice-ball until another ship arrives. That is, unless I can . . . shall we say, *convince* . . . your cute little Asian officer to cooperate . . ."

VanDeese roared and charged the man from behind, the solid rod held tightly in his hands. The startled scientist spun around, the flame carving a blinding blue arc in the darkness. Shelkop's right hand holding the tank swept wide, allowing the captain to strike him squarely in the chest with the length of the pole. VanDeese leaped back as the scientist screamed and slashed again with the propane tank, its flame just missing the captain's face. VanDeese brought up his left hand, jabbing the pole into Shelkop's right side just below the ribs. The scientist doubled over and dropped the torch to the floor. As the captain was about to finish his follow-through by bringing the pole in his right hand down, the scientist anticipated the move and turned to deflect the blow onto his left shoulder.

Shelkop lunged forward, catching VanDeese in the stomach. He propelled them both across the room and slammed the captain against a rack of extruded pipes nearly two meters in diameter. VanDeese was stunned just long enough for Shelkop to wrench the rod from his hands. The scientist gripped the pole with both hands and swung it over his head. He brought the pole down in an axe-chop but the captain dodged to his left, managing to escape the blow. The *Syntax* rod made a loud *THONG!* on the pipes as it hit, just missing the captain's head.

VanDeese dived for the fallen propane tank, grabbing it in his right hand and rolling onto his back. The blue flame sliced through the darkness between the two men. The scientist swung the pole down, hitting the captain's wrist, sending the torch skidding across the floor and under the rack of long, huge-diameter pipes. Shelkop shifted his grip on the rod to use it as a spear and jabbed it at the floor around the captain's head. In the darkened room he could only approximate VanDeese's location, giving the captain time to roll himself under a nearby table.

VanDeese pressed as tightly as he could into the small space under the table as the scientist struck furiously with the pole. Suddenly behind them, there was the sound of a bullwhip *THWAP!* as one of the nylon retaining straps on one end of the rack of enormous *Syntax* pipes was severed by the burning flame of the fallen propane tank.

The startled scientist reeled around to the noise behind him, brandishing the pole like a spear. Captain VanDeese took the brief moment to grope in his boot for the sedative ampule. He pulled it free and stabbed it into the darkness, striking Shelkop in the right leg just above the ankle.

The scientist cried out in pain and fury and began to stagger across the room, the sedative already taking effect. He stumbled and fell across the stack of large-diameter pipes, their ends shifting under the extra weight. The awkward angle of the skewed pipes proved too much for the single remaining nylon strap, causing it to snap instantly.

Doctor Shelkop reeled drunkenly and screamed as the pile of giant pipes cascaded down over themselves, crushing and silencing the psychotic scientist. VanDeese pressed his body tighter within the tiny space below the table as the large *Syntax* tubes bounced and slammed against his protective cubbyhole. The thundering vibrations shook the floor and the captain's body, their sounds echoing from the walls and into the adjoining rooms, eventually fading, leaving only a loud ringing in the captain's ears. That, too, gradually diminished and faded to nothingness.

He was floating.

His limbs felt weightless as he drifted upward from the dark depths to what he perceived to be the surface. Drifting, rising, floating. He didn't struggle, nor did he strain to propel himself and hurry his ascension. He just let go and allowed his body to relax and drift.

There was a light above, like the shimmering diffused refraction of a smooth water's surface. He felt calm and serene, at peace with his surroundings – and with himself.

So this is what death is like . . .

He heard voices. They were garbled and indistinct, but VanDeese soon became aware enough to understand words and phrases. It was an exchange between a man and a woman, not speaking to him, but to each other. The woman's voice was saying, "If you don't stop fidgeting around, I can't do a proper patching job. I have restraining devices for my more difficult and uncooperative patients."

"All right, *Madame DeSade*," the man's voice answered. "Just watch where you're waving that thing."

Not death. Life.

Continue with his life . . .

Wonderful, joyous, precious life.

His life.

VanDeese opened his eyes and turned his head. *The Saint* was sitting restlessly on a stool as Bettye Yale closed his scalp wound with a laser-suture. "Hey there, Ron," the captain croaked in a raspy voice. His mouth and throat felt dry. "How are we feeling?"

"Fine, just fine," the engineer retorted sarcastically. "We'll be even better when *Zorro* here is through brandishing her laser-saber."

Bettye shook her head and made a clicking sound with her tongue. "Men," she exclaimed in exasperation. "You're all a bunch of babies."

"You could use a little refresher course on your bedside manner," Ron growled under his breath.

The captain raised himself onto one elbow and looked around the infirmary. "I take it," he said flatly, "that Shelkop is dead."

Doctor Yale turned and faced him. "I've seldom seen anyone deader," she admitted dryly. "Pardon me if I don't get all teary-eyed over his passing."

VanDeese swung his legs over the edge of the observation table and raised himself to a sitting position. His head felt clearer and there was only a little stiffness, probably from wedging himself beneath that table. "So how did I get here?"

Ron smiled. "Our lady doctor here thought you may need some help when your readout started going flickety. So she called MeGill who found me and gave me a hand. He and I hooked the pipes to the ceiling winch and pulled you free." The engineer cocked his head and furrowed his brow. "Funny thing," he said. "You weren't hurt a bit. We found you sleeping like a baby."

"No surpise," the captain exhaled, stretching his arms over his head. "That was one time my slumber wasn't prematurely interrupted."

"They brought you in here so I could keep an eye on you until you woke up," Bettye explained. She crossed over to him and pointed a slim finger at the captain's chest. "Catching a nap in a cramped mouse hole does not constitute rest and relaxation. I *still* insist that you get more sleep than you have been." She placed her hands on her hips and regarded him sternly. "*Doctors orders,*" she stated authoritatively.

VanDeese raised his palms in defense. "All right, I surrender!" he smiled. "Just let me make a quick inspection of the bridge and see how Lieutenant Soo is getting along." Doctor Yale's expression told him she was unconvinced. "Just the bridge, that's all. I promise."

The physician's face softened a fraction. "Okay," she conceded warily. "But then it's off to bed." She began to turn away, then gave him a glaring glance over her shoulder. "*Alone.*" She wagged her thin finger in his face. "Remember, you can't hide the truth from me, so do as you're told."

The captain soberly saluted the woman and hopped down from the table. "Yes ma'am."

Li Soo looked up from her science console as the doors of the *tube* slid open and VanDeese stepped onto the bridge. "Captain," she lilted happily offering a warm smile. "I'm glad to see that you're all right."

VanDeese took two steps toward his command chair, then turned to see the front view screen. The display glowed with the deep scarlet and crimson hues from their close proximity to the Red Giant, Jupiter. The swirling eddies and currents of its immense dark eye nearly filled the screen.

"Magnificent, isn't it?" Lieutenant Soo asked in a hushed voice.

The captain stared in awe for a moment, admiring its beauty. "I never expected it to be so incredible. It's utterly fantastic!" He slowly stepped backwards into his chair and sat down, his eyes still riveted to the amazing view.

He sat facing the front display in silence for a long while. The stirring, churning movements of the storms and currents were both relaxing and fascinating to watch. The great planet reflected the swirling thoughts within his own mind, the opposing forces clashing within his brain. VanDeese was relieved that the crisis was not a case of ship-wide dementia – only the mad ravings of a power-hungry lunatic. Shelkop saw in these abandoned, unwanted children the opportunity of unlimited potential, though solely for his own benefit, not theirs. It was ironic that Earth's rejected refuse would become superior to those who would cast them into oblivion.

VanDeese felt a wave of relief in the realization that one churning roiling storm had finally subsided –

the tempest within him regarding his anxiety over losing his beloved Jenny. Somehow he knew she was at peace, that he should no longer bear the torment and despair over her loss nor the guilt in wanting to desire intimacy with another woman. He could allow himself to feel again – to love again.

To continue with his life.

The captain silently chastised himself for nearly succumbing to the temptation of playing God with this new race of beings. No single person should hold the destiny of an entire species in the palm of his hand. Mankind had already driven many of Earth's species to extinction through ignorance or arrogance. VanDeese had no right to decide the fate of this newest facet of humanity.

"I've been giving some thought to this mind-probing business," he mused absently, as if only to himself. "I'll need to have a talk with Doctor Garcia. She may be a government official, but she's still a doctor and a scientist. She'll have to make sure the embryos are raised and trained properly and not have their abilities abused or exploited." VanDeese stroked his chin and shrugged his shoulders. "Who knows," he conceded. "Perhaps this is the next step in human evolution."

They both sat in silence, watching the swirling eddying colors on the forward view screen. At last, VanDeese expelled a long breath. "As for the adults," he sighed. "They're just going to have to learn to live with it."

Li Soo slowly rose to her feet and quietly stepped behind the captain's chair, bending low and draping her arms around his neck. "Which reminds me," she whispered into his ear. "You never *did* give me an honest answer to the question that I put to you when we were alone in the *tube* together."

"I didn't?"

"No," she cooed, her lips brushing his lobe. "You didn't."

VanDeese smiled and slowly reached up with his hand and grasped her elbow. He gently pulled the young woman around and into his lap. "Isn't it obvious?" he grinned. "I had thought that even *you* could read the answer in my eyes."

The two pressed their lips together in a growing passionate embrace, neither paying attention to the door of the *tube* as it slid open. *The Saint* smiled warmly as he spotted the two lovers, folding his arms across his big chest and allowing the door to close silently upon him once more.

www.ingramcontent.com/pod-product-compliance
Ingram Content Group UK Ltd.
Pitfield, Milton Keynes, MK11 3LW, UK
UKHW040015200726
13854UKWH00001B/217

9 781403 389176